SUPER EASY SONGBOOK

HIT SONGS

ISBN 978-1-4950-7327-4

HAL•LEONARD®

7777 W. BLUEMOUND RD. P.O. BOX 13819 MILWAUKEE, WI 53213

Visit Hal Leonard Online at
www.halleonard.com

Welcome to the *Super Easy Songbook* series!

This unique collection will help you play your favorite songs quickly and easily. Here's how it works:

- Play the simplified melody with your right hand. Letter names appear inside each note to assist you.

- There are no key signatures to worry about! If a sharp ♯ or flat ♭ is needed, it is shown beside the note each time.

- There are no page turns, so your hands never have to leave the keyboard.

- If two notes are connected by a tie ‿, hold the first note for the combined number of beats. (The second note does not show a letter name since it is not re-struck.)

- Add basic chords with your left hand using the provided keyboard diagrams. Chord voicings have been carefully chosen to minimize hand movement.

- The left-hand rhythm is up to you, and chord notes can be played together or separately. Be creative!

- If the chords sound muddy, move your left hand an octave* higher. If this gets in the way of playing the melody, move your right hand an octave higher as well.

   * *An octave spans eight notes. If your starting note is C, the next C to the right is an octave higher.*

—————————————— ALSO AVAILABLE ——————————————

Hal Leonard Student Keyboard Guide HL00296039

Key Stickers HL00100016

The A Team

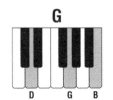
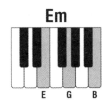
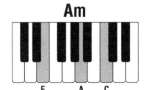
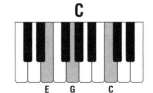
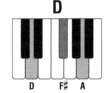

Words and Music by
Ed Sheeran

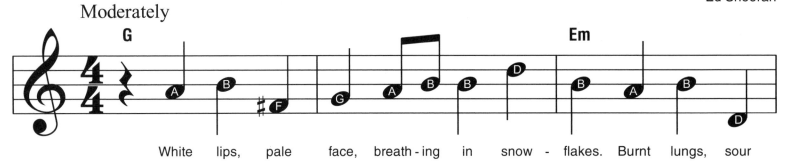

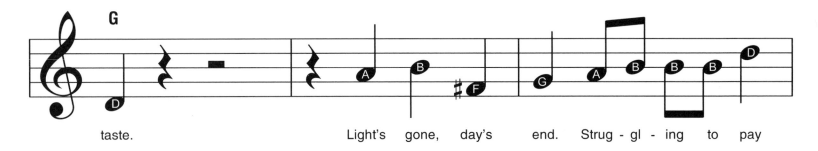

White lips, pale face, breath-ing in snow-flakes. Burnt lungs, sour

taste. Light's gone, day's end. Strug-gl-ing to pay

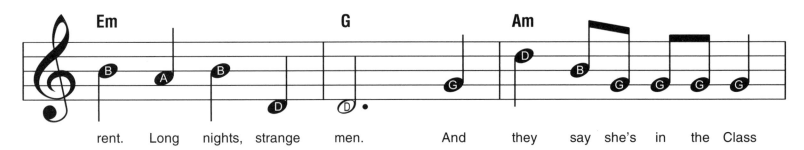

rent. Long nights, strange men. And they say she's in the Class

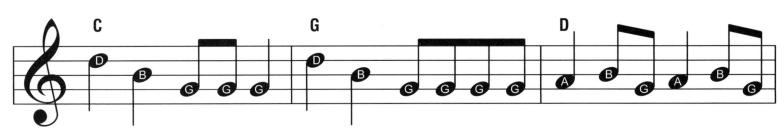

A team. Stuck in her day-dream. Been this way since eight-een, but late-ly her

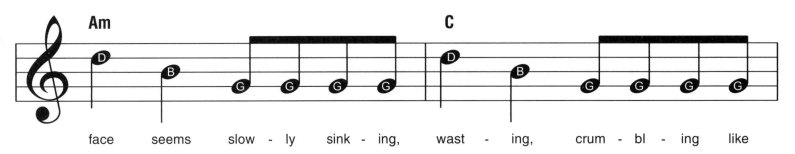

face seems slow-ly sink-ing, wast-ing, crum-bl-ing like

All About That Bass

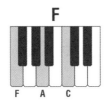
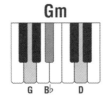
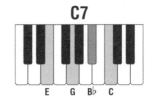

Words and Music by Kevin Kadish
and Meghan Trainor

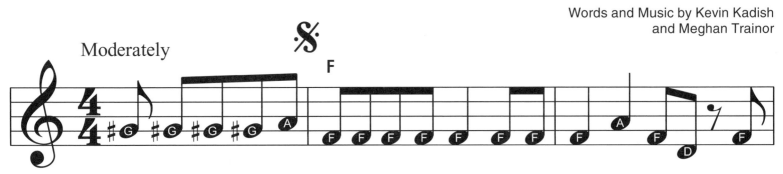

Be - cause you know I'm all a - bout that bass, 'bout that bass. No tre - ble. I'm

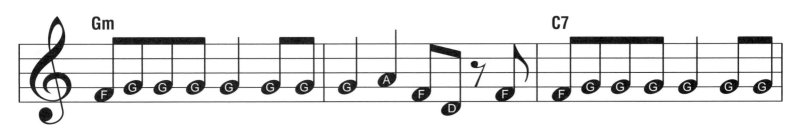

all a - bout that bass, 'bout that bass. No tre - ble. I'm all a - bout that bass, 'bout that

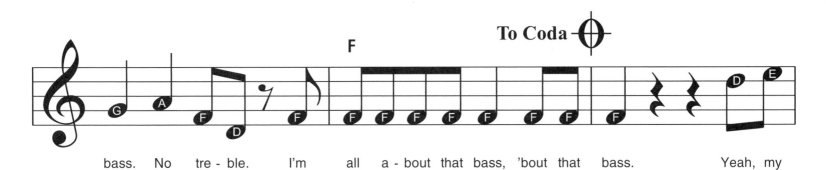

bass. No tre - ble. I'm all a - bout that bass, 'bout that bass. Yeah, my

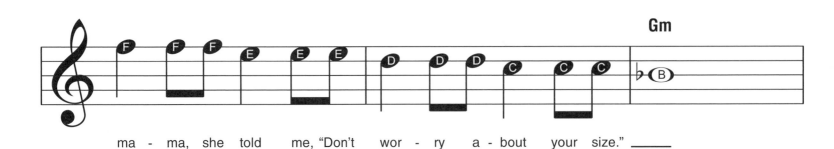

ma - ma, she told me, "Don't wor - ry a - bout your size." _____

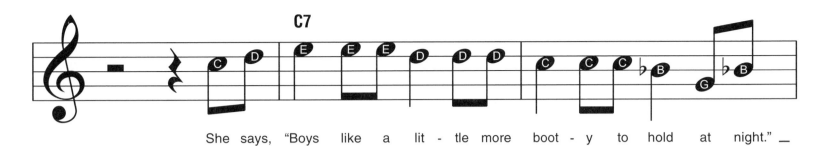

She says, "Boys like a lit - tle more boot - y to hold at night." __

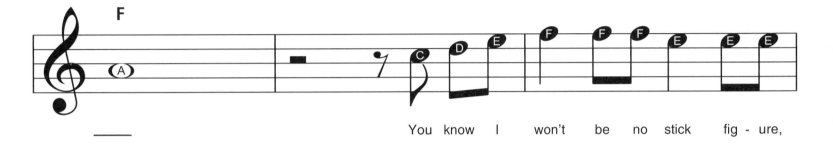

__ You know I won't be no stick fig - ure,

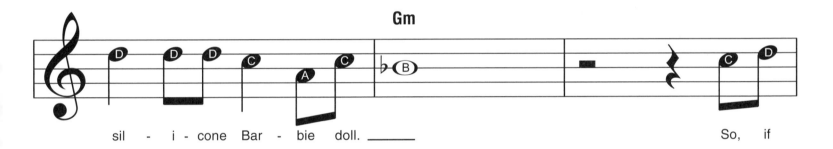

sil - i - cone Bar - bie doll. _____ So, if

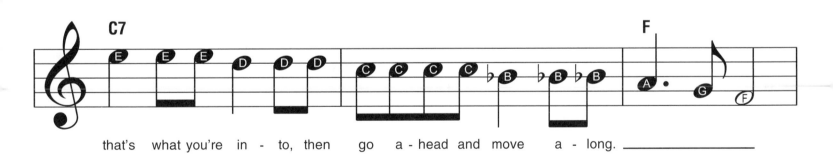

that's what you're in - to, then go a - head and move a - long. _____

D.S. al Coda
(Return to 𝄋, play to ⨁
and skip to Coda)

CODA

Be - cause you know I'm   bass.

All of Me

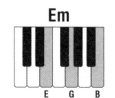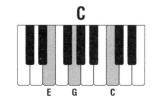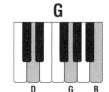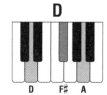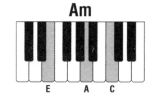

Words and Music by John Stephens
and Toby Gad

Moderately slow

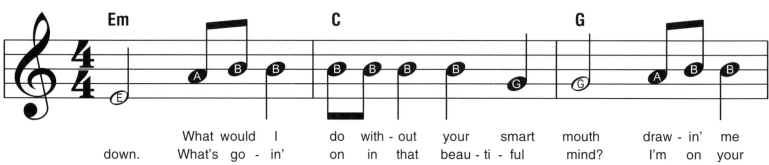

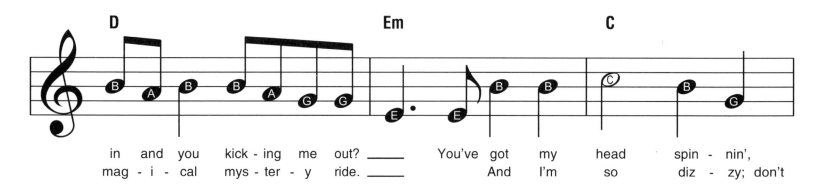

What would I do with-out your smart mouth draw-in' me
down. What's go-in' on in that beau-ti-ful mind? I'm on your

in and you kick-ing me out? _____ You've got my head spin-nin',
mag-i-cal mys-ter-y ride. _____ And I'm so diz-zy; don't

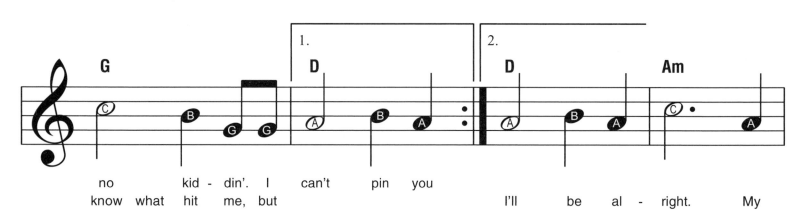

no kid-din'. I can't pin you
know what hit me, but

I'll be al-right. My

head's un-der wa-ter, but I'm breath-ing fine.

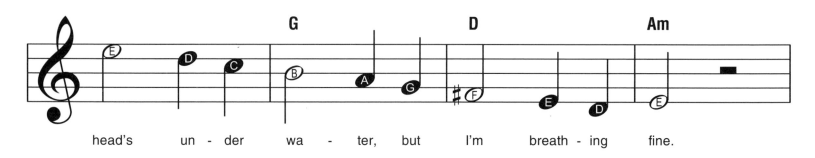

Apologize

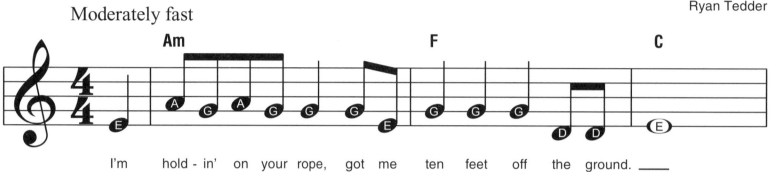

Words and Music by
Ryan Tedder

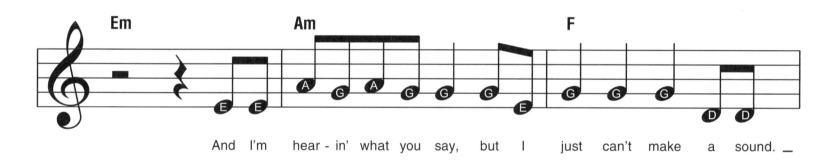

I'm hold-in' on your rope, got me ten feet off the ground. ____

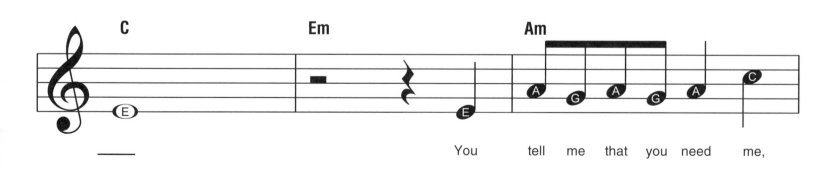

And I'm hear-in' what you say, but I just can't make a sound. _

You tell me that you need me,

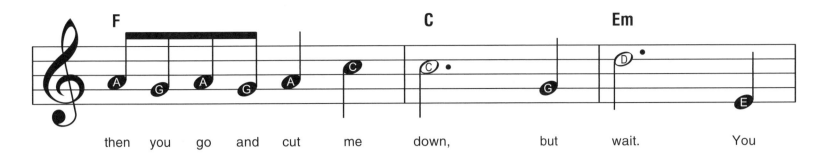

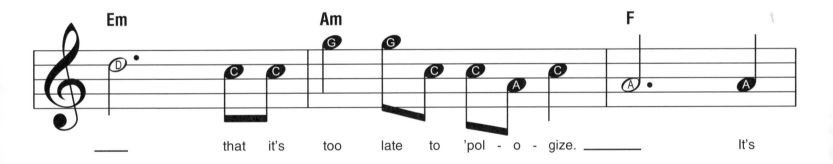

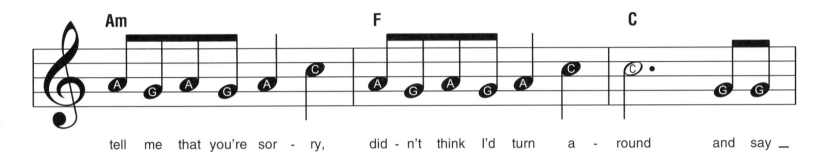

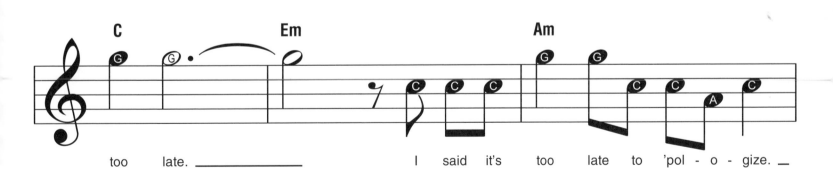

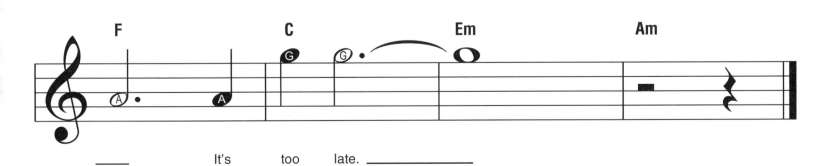

Blurred Lines

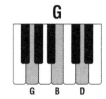
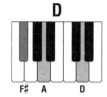

Words and Music by Pharrell Williams,
Robin Thicke and Clifford Harris

Moderate groove

You're a good girl. I know you want it. I know you want it.

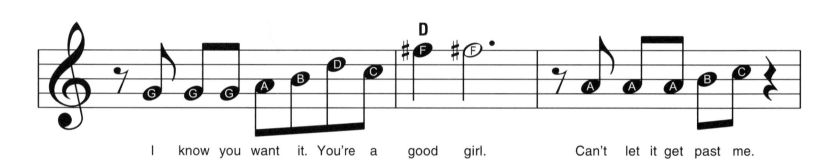

I know you want it. You're a good girl. Can't let it get past me.

You're far from plas - tic. Talk a - bout get - tin' blast - ed. I hate these

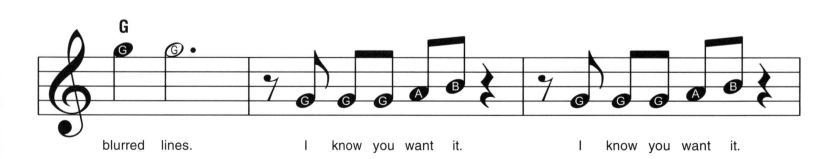

blurred lines. I know you want it. I know you want it.

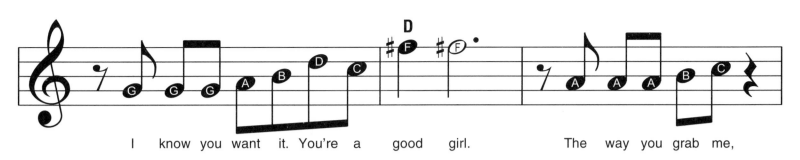

I know you want it. You're a good girl. The way you grab me,

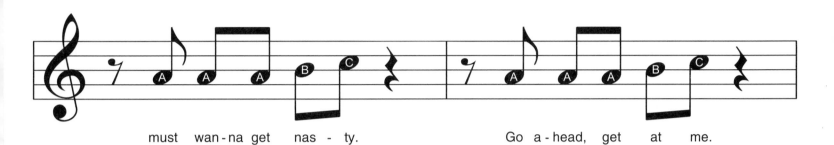

must wan-na get nas-ty. Go a-head, get at me.

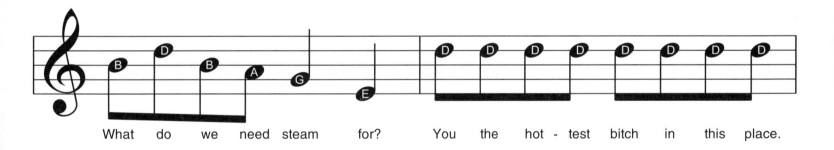

What do they make dreams for when you got them jeans on?

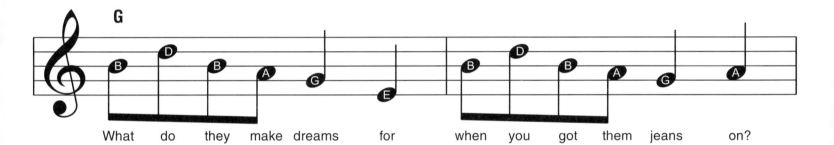

What do we need steam for? You the hot-test bitch in this place.

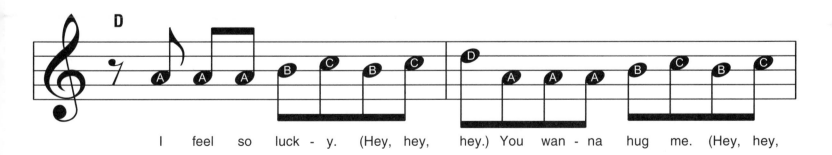

I feel so luck-y. (Hey, hey, hey.) You wan-na hug me. (Hey, hey,

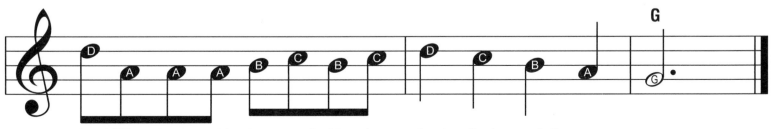

hey.) What rhymes with hug me? (Hey, hey, hey.) *(Instrumental)*

Brave

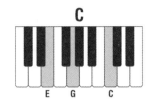 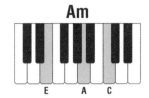 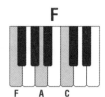 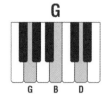

Words and Music by Sara Bareilles
and Jack Antonoff

Moderately

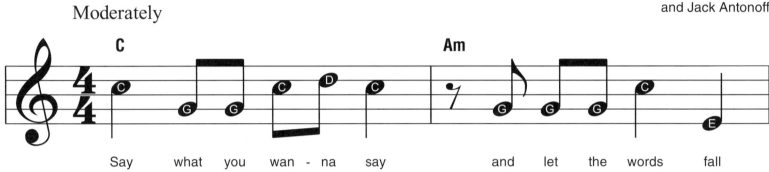

Say what you wan - na say and let the words fall

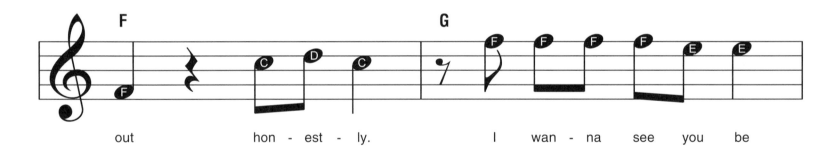

out hon - est - ly. I wan - na see you be

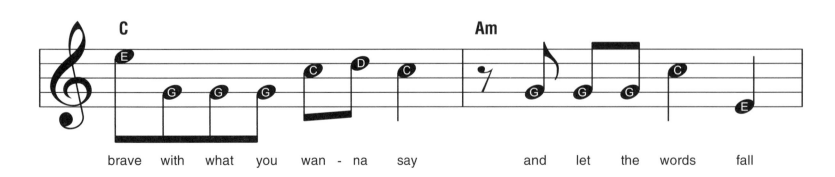

brave with what you wan - na say and let the words fall

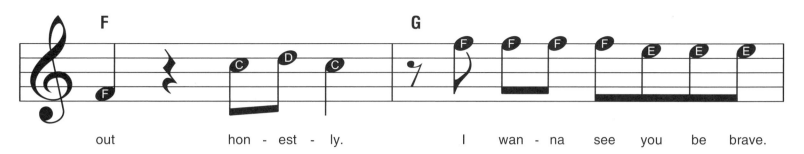

out   hon - est - ly.   I   wan - na   see   you   be   brave.

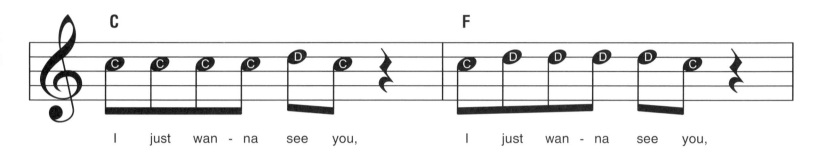

I   just   wan - na   see   you,   I   just   wan - na   see   you,

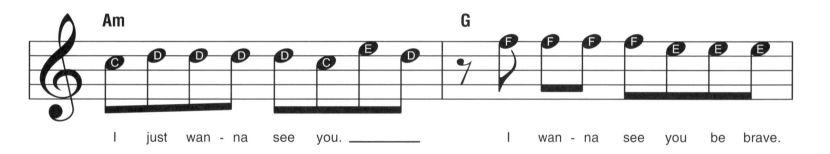

I   just   wan - na   see   you. _____   I   wan - na   see   you   be   brave.

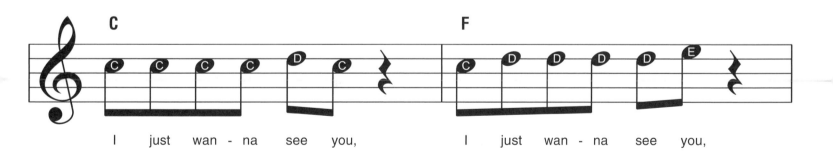

I   just   wan - na   see   you,   I   just   wan - na   see   you,

I   just wan - na   see   you. _____   I   wan - na   see   you   be   brave.

Budapest

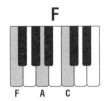
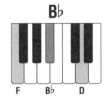
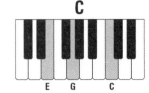

Words and Music by George Barnett
and Joel Pott

Moderately fast

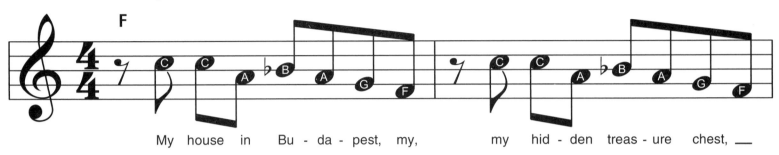

My house in Bu - da - pest, my, my hid - den treas - ure chest, ___

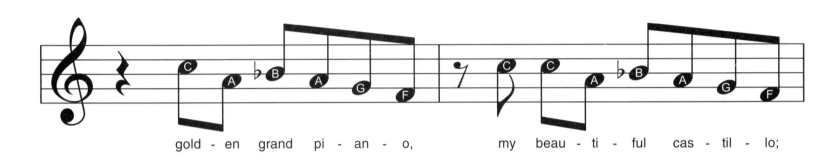

gold - en grand pi - an - o, my beau - ti - ful cas - til - lo;

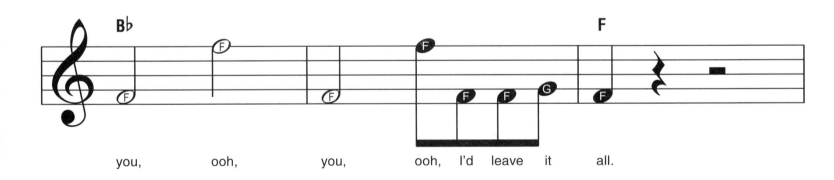

you, ooh, you, ooh, I'd leave it all.

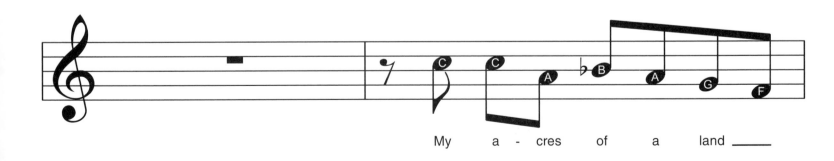

My a - cres of a land ___

19

Call Me Maybe

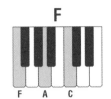 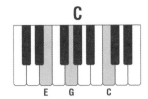 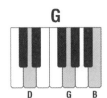 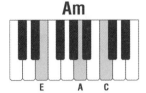

Words and Music by Carly Rae Jepsen,
Joshua Ramsay and Tavish Crowe

Moderately fast

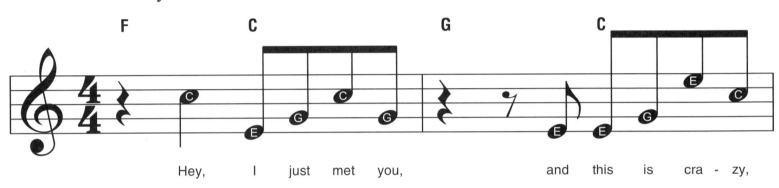

Hey, I just met you, and this is cra - zy,

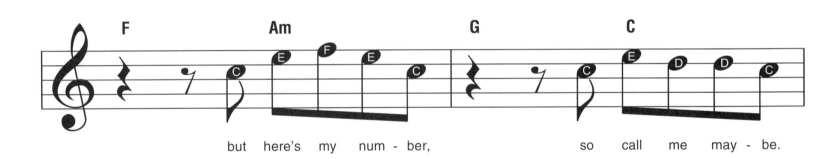

but here's my num - ber, so call me may - be.

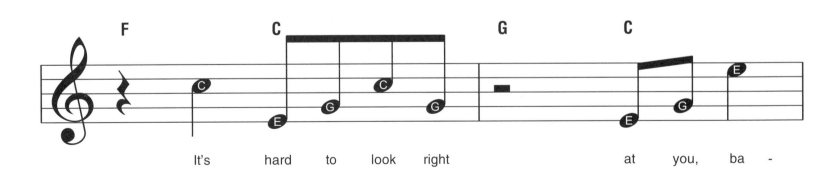

It's hard to look right at you, ba -

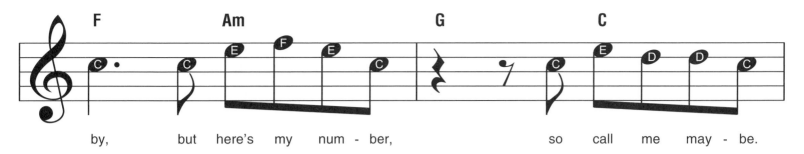

by, but here's my num - ber, so call me may - be.

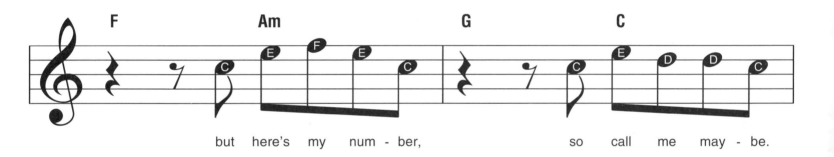

Hey, I just met you, and this is cra - zy,

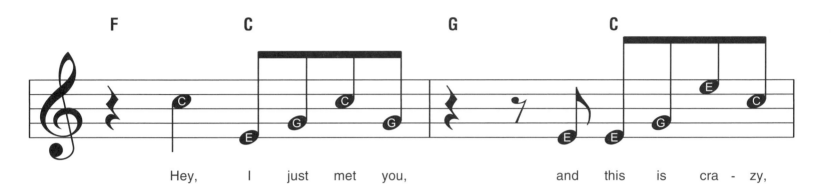

but here's my num - ber, so call me may - be.

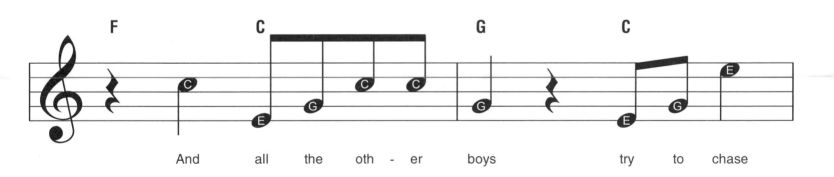

And all the oth - er boys try to chase

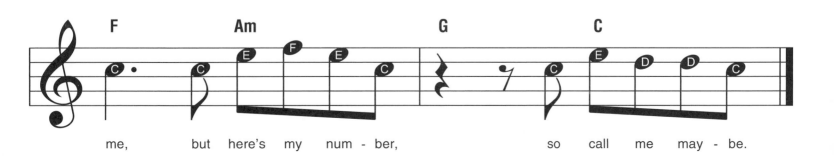

me, but here's my num - ber, so call me may - be.

Can't Feel My Face

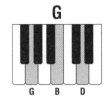 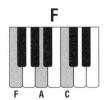 

Words and Music by Abel Tesfaye,
Max Martin, Savan Kotecha,
Peter Svensson and Ali Payami

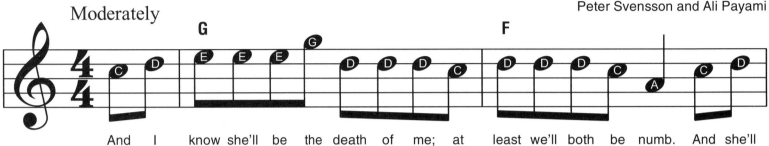

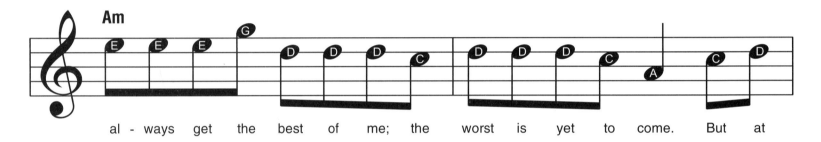

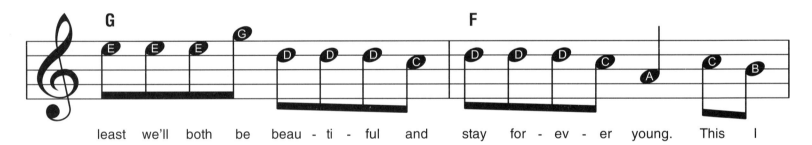

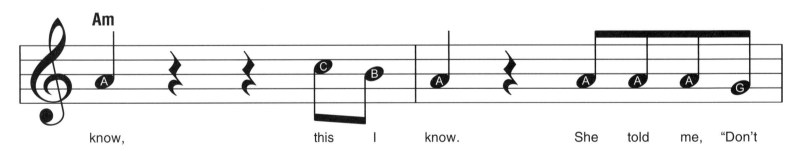

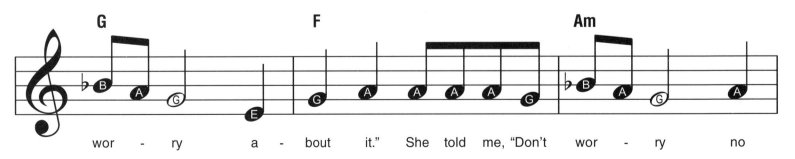

Can't Stop the Feeling
from TROLLS

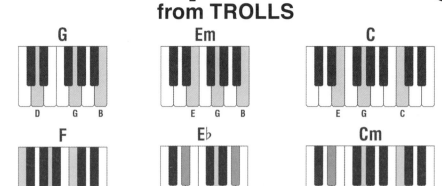

Words and Music by Justin Timberlake,
Max Martin and Shellback

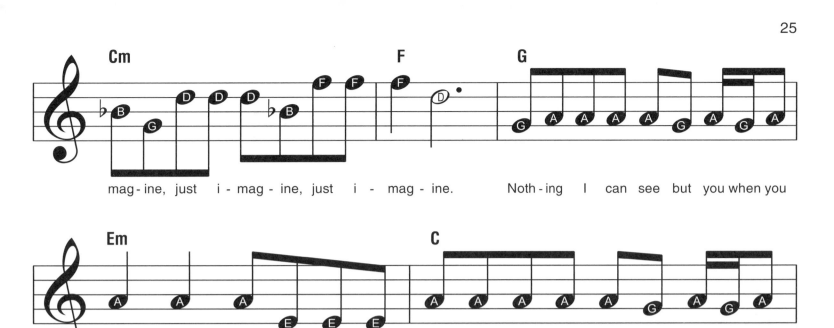

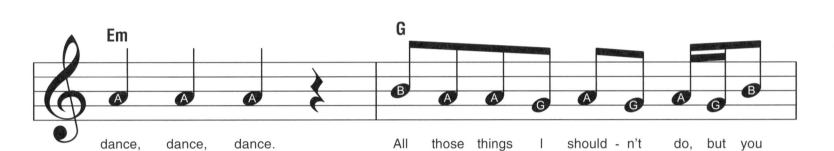

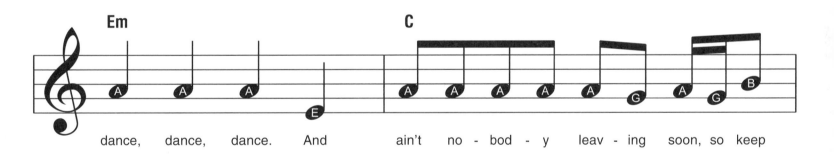

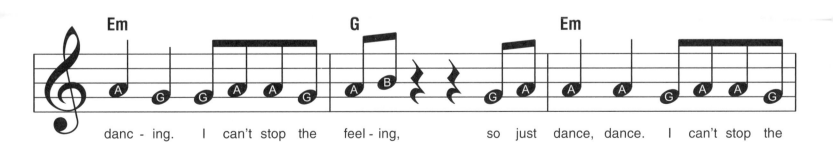

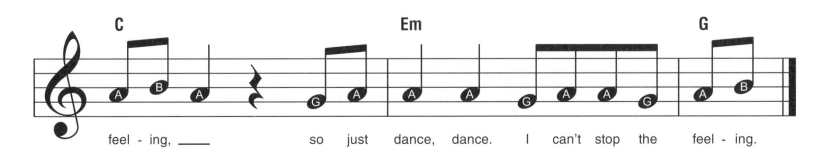

Chasing Cars

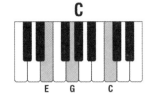 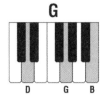 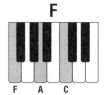

Words and Music by Gary Lightbody,
Tom Simpson, Paul Wilson,
Jonathan Quinn and Nathan Connolly

27

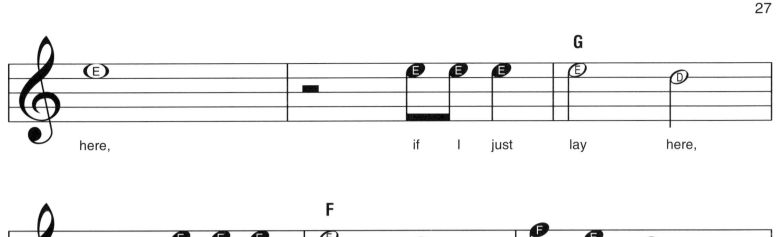

here,   if I just lay here,

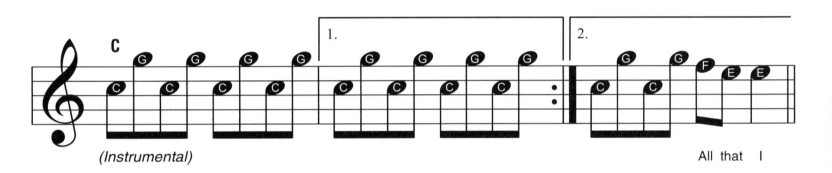

would you lie with me and just for - get the world?

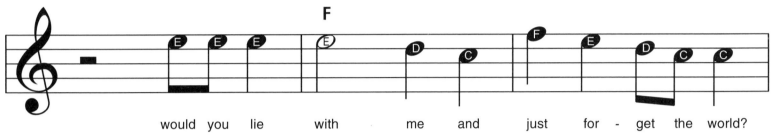

(Instrumental)   All that I

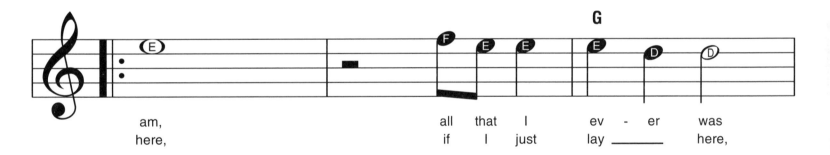

am,   all that I ev - er was
here,   if I just lay _____ here,

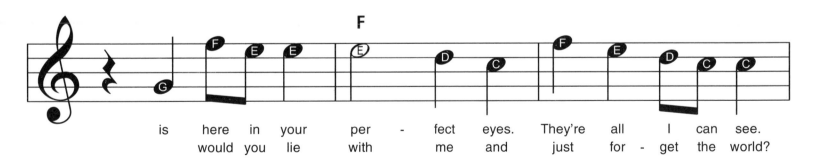

is here in your per - fect eyes. They're all I can see.
would you lie with me and just for - get the world?

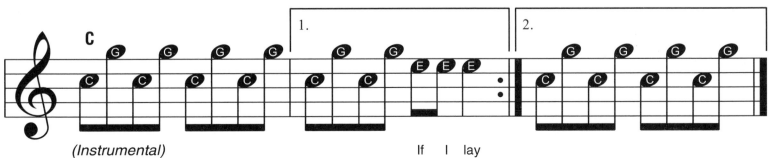

(Instrumental)   If I lay

Ex's & Oh's

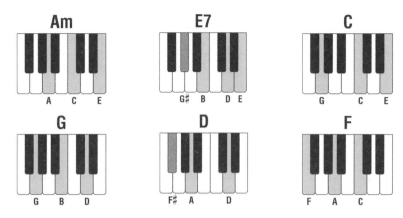

Words and Music by Tanner Schneider
and Dave Bassett

Moderately fast Shuffle

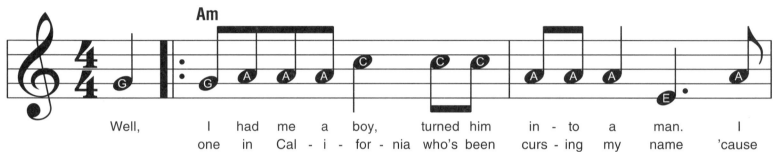

Well, I had me a boy, turned him in-to a man. I
one in Cal-i-for-nia who's been curs-ing my name 'cause

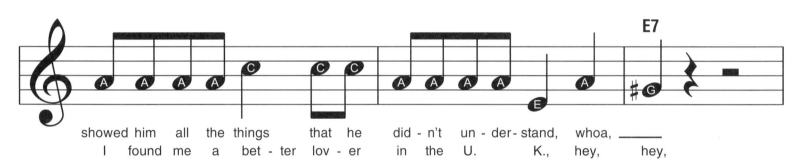

showed him all the things that he did-n't un-der-stand, whoa, _____
I found me a bet-ter lov-er in the U. K., hey, hey,

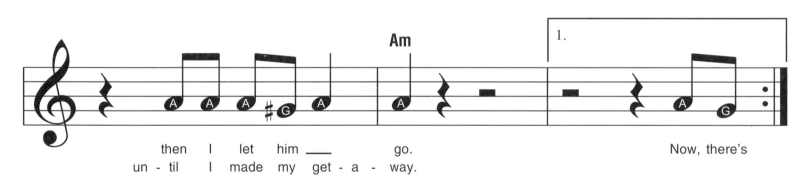

then I let him ___ go.
un-til I made my get-a-way.

Now, there's

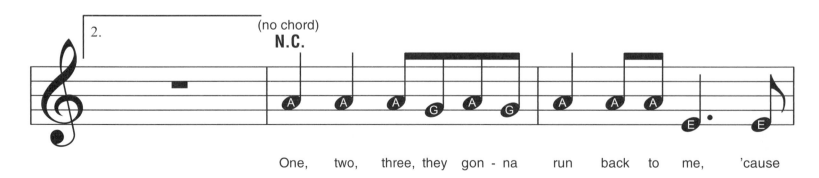

One, two, three, they gon-na run back to me, 'cause

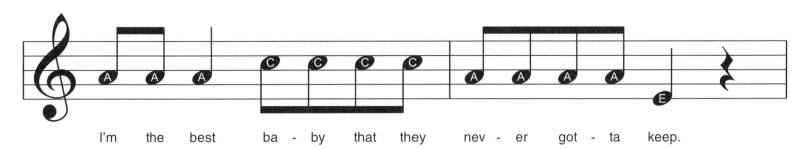

I'm the best ba - by that they nev - er got - ta keep.

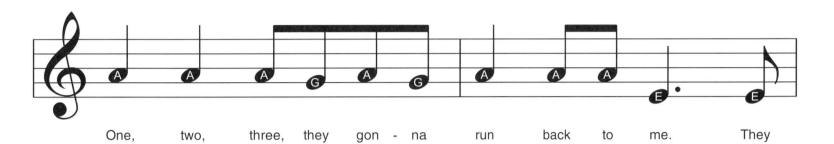

One, two, three, they gon - na run back to me. They

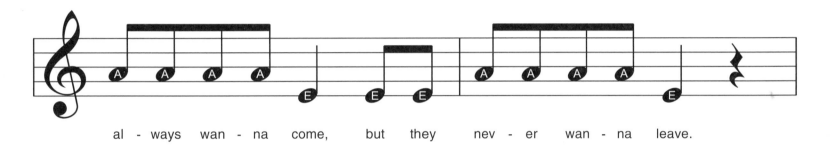

al - ways wan - na come, but they nev - er wan - na leave.

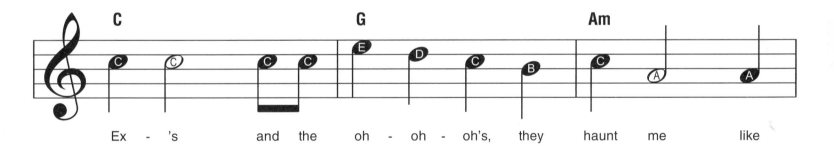

Ex - 's and the oh - oh - oh's, they haunt me like

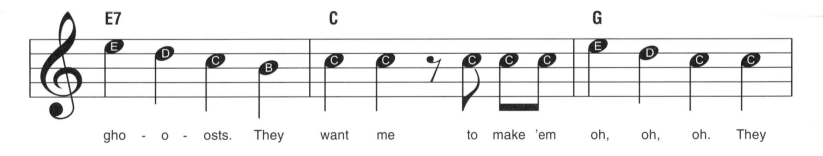

gho - o - osts. They want me to make 'em oh, oh, oh. They

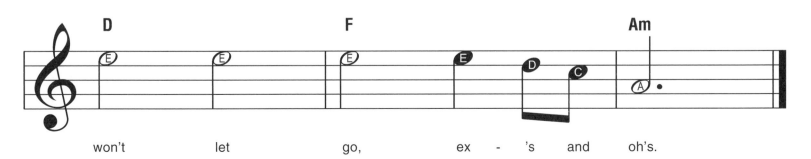

won't let go, ex - 's and oh's.

Forget You

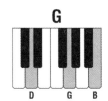 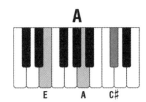 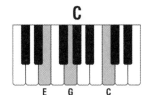 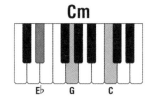

Words and Music by Bruno Mars,
Ari Levine, Philip Lawrence,
Thomas Callaway and Brody Brown

Moderately

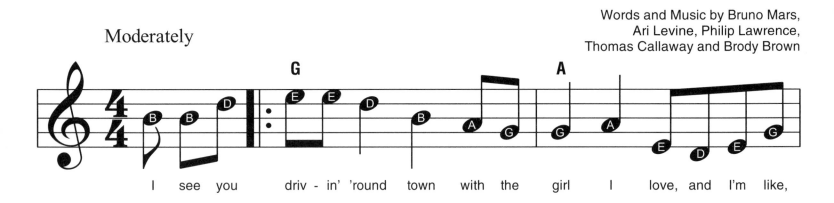

I see you driv-in' 'round town with the girl I love, and I'm like,

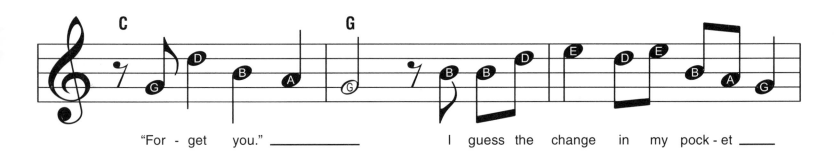

"For-get you." ____ I guess the change in my pock-et ____

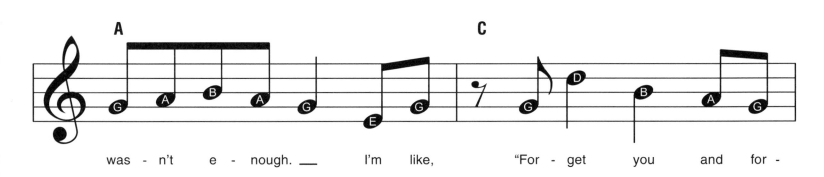

was-n't e-nough. __ I'm like, "For-get you and for-

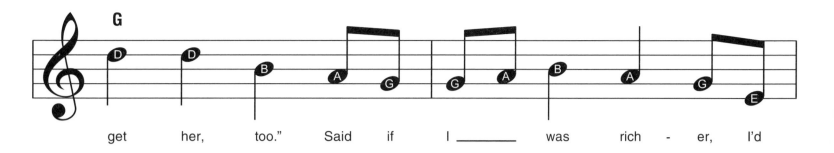

get her, too." Said if I _____ was rich - er, I'd

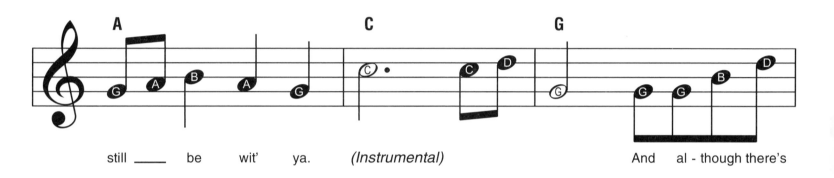

still ____ be wit' ya. *(Instrumental)* And al - though there's

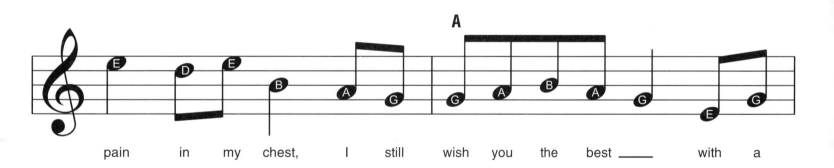

pain in my chest, I still wish you the best ____ with a

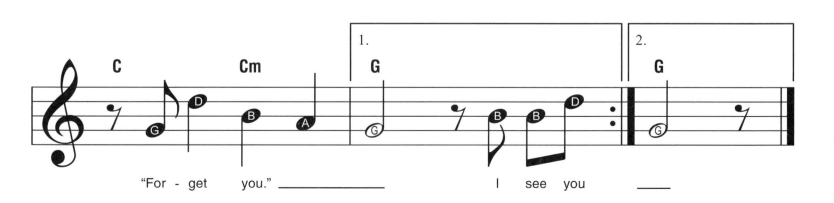

"For - get you." _____ I see you ____

Get Lucky

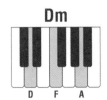
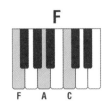
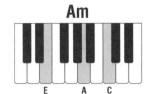
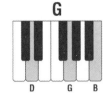

Words and Music by Thomas Bangalter,
Guy Manuel Homem Christo, Nile Rodgers
and Pharrell Williams

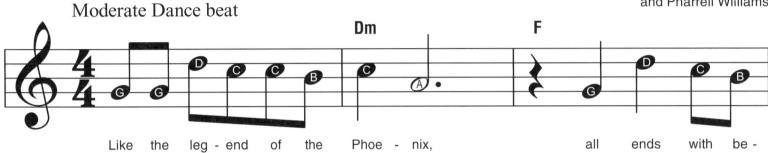

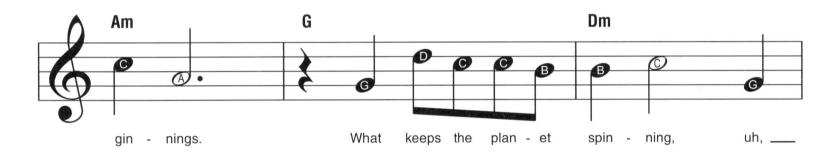

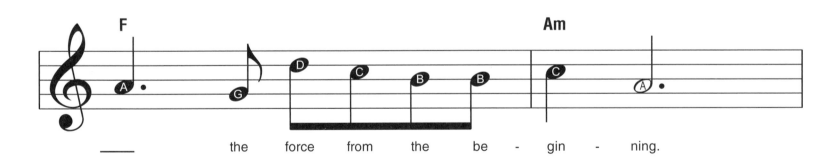

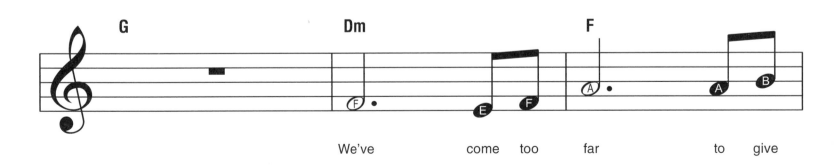

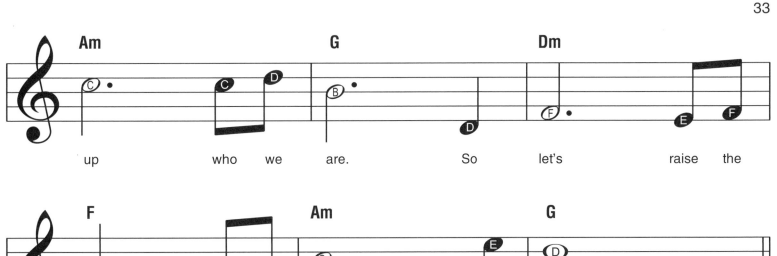

up   who we are.   So   let's   raise   the

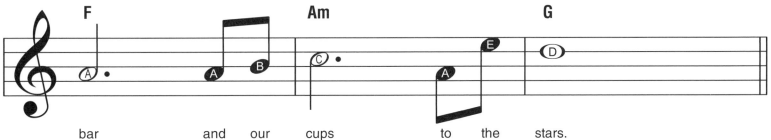

bar   and our cups   to the stars.

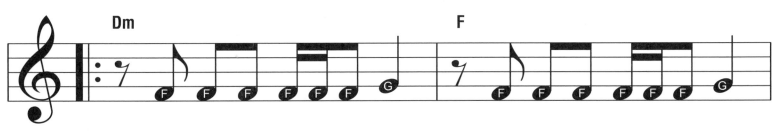

She's up all night till the sun.   I'm up all night to get some.

We're up all night till the sun.   We're up all night to get some.

She's up all night for good fun.   I'm up all night to get luck - y.

We're up all night for good fun.   We're up all night to get luck - y.

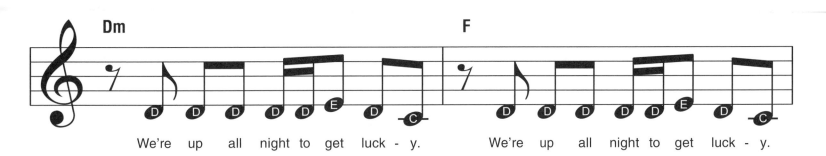

We're up all night to get luck - y.   We're up all night to get luck - y.

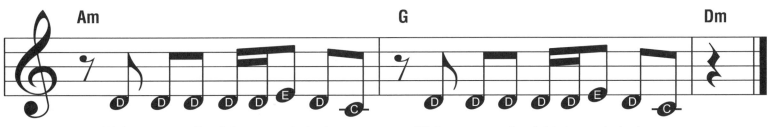

We're up all night to get luck - y.   We're up all night to get luck - y.

Happy
from DESPICABLE ME 2

Words and Music by
Pharrell Williams

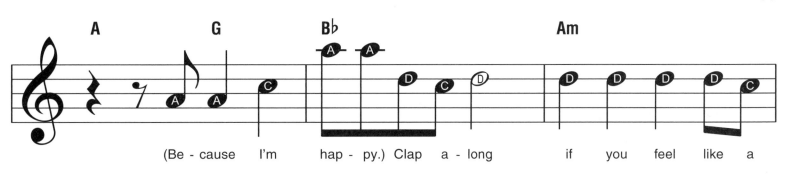

(Be - cause I'm hap - py.) Clap a - long if you feel like a

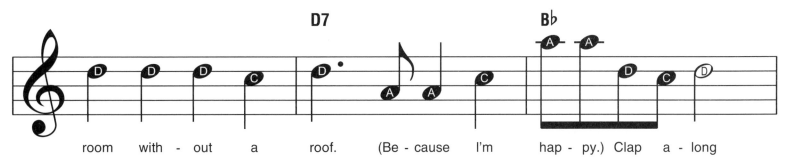

room with - out a roof. (Be - cause I'm hap - py.) Clap a - long

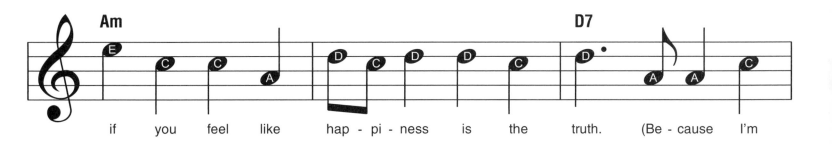

if you feel like hap - pi - ness is the truth. (Be - cause I'm

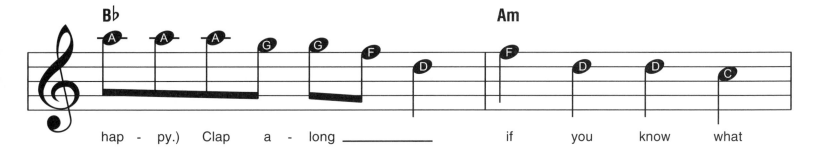

hap - py.) Clap a - long _____ if you know what

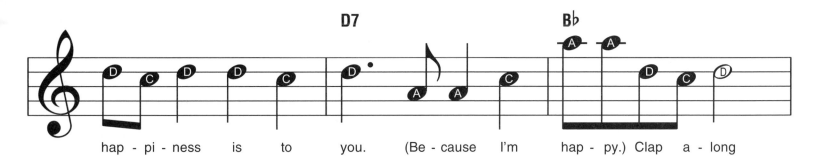

hap - pi - ness is to you. (Be - cause I'm hap - py.) Clap a - long

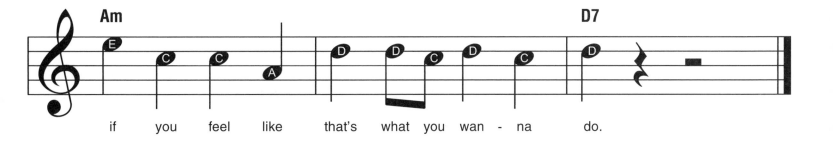

if you feel like that's what you wan - na do.

Hello

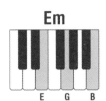
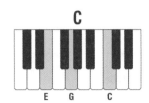
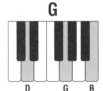
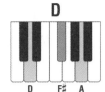

Words and Music by Adele Adkins
and Greg Kurstin

Moderately slow

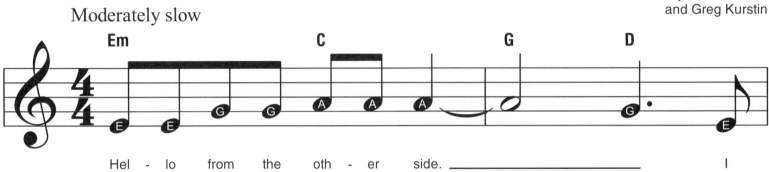

Hel - lo from the oth - er side. _____ I

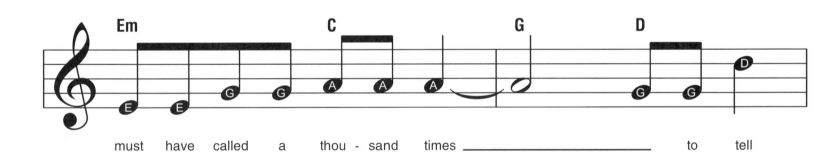

must have called a thou - sand times _____ to tell

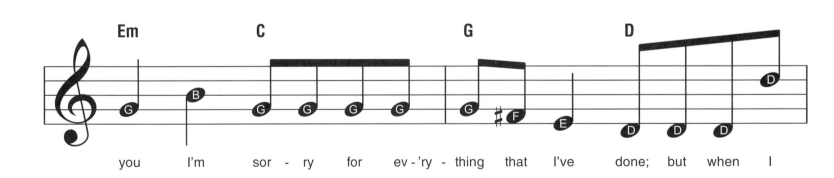

you I'm sor - ry for ev - 'ry - thing that I've done; but when I

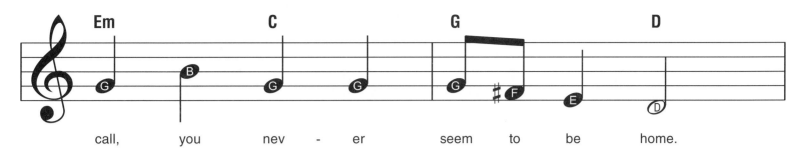

call, you nev - er seem to be home.

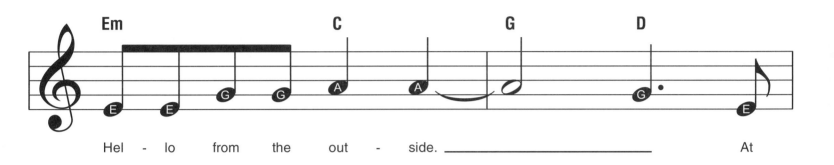

Hel - lo from the out - side. _____ At

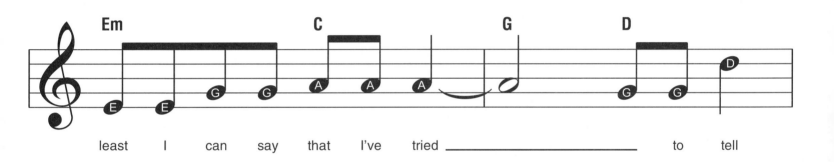

least I can say that I've tried _____ to tell

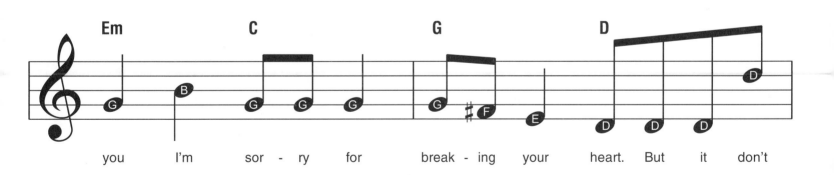

you I'm sor - ry for break - ing your heart. But it don't

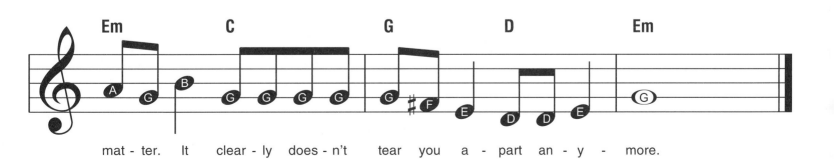

mat - ter. It clear - ly does - n't tear you a - part an - y - more.

Hey, Soul Sister

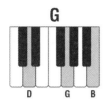
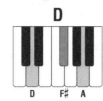
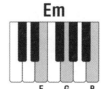
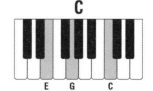

Words and Music by Pat Monahan,
Espen Lind and Amund Bjorklund

Moderately

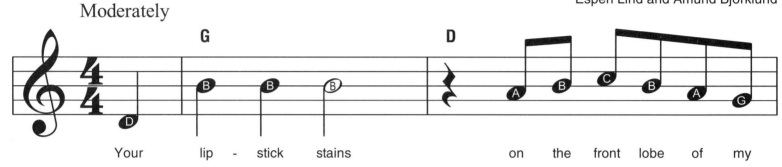

Your lip - stick stains on the front lobe of my

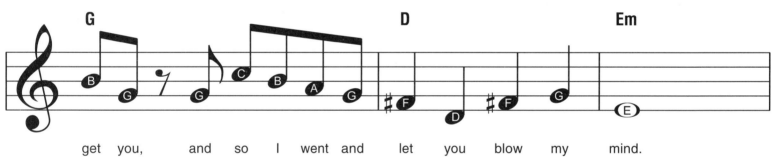

left - side brains. I knew I would - n't for -

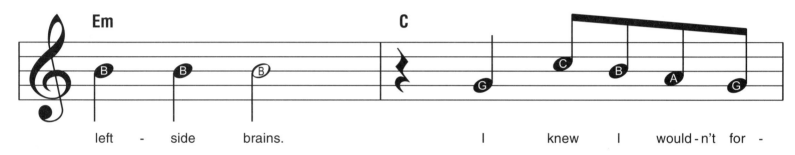

get you, and so I went and let you blow my mind.

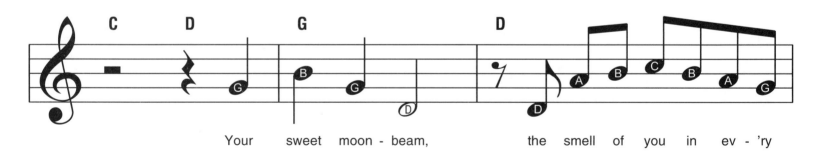

Your sweet moon - beam, the smell of you in ev - 'ry

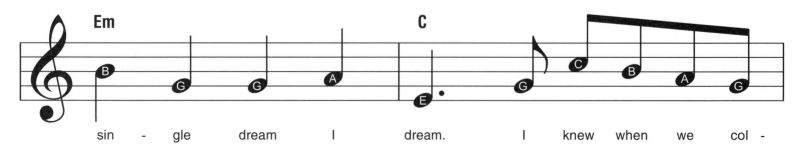

sin - gle dream I dream. I knew when we col -

Hey There Delilah

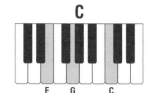 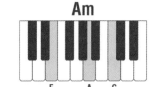 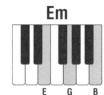 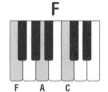 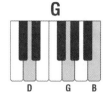

Words and Music by
Tom Higgenson

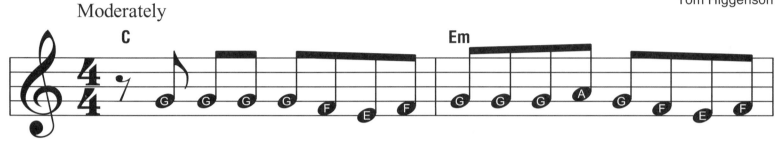

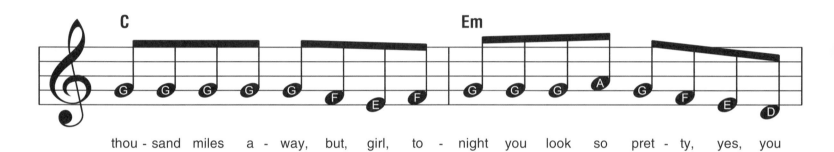

Hey there, De - li - lah, what's it like in New York Cit - y? I'm a

thou - sand miles a - way, but, girl, to - night you look so pret - ty, yes, you

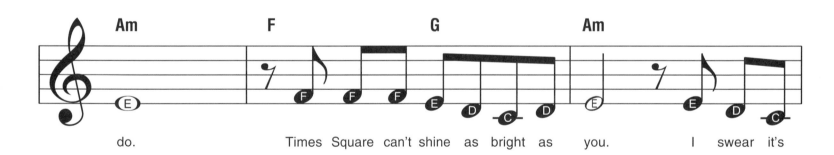

do. Times Square can't shine as bright as you. I swear it's

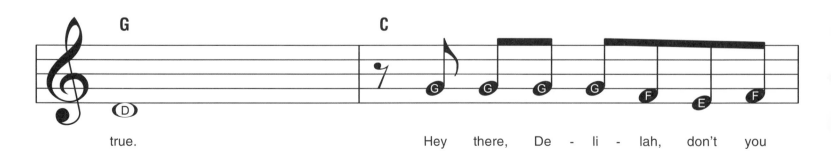

true. Hey there, De - li - lah, don't you

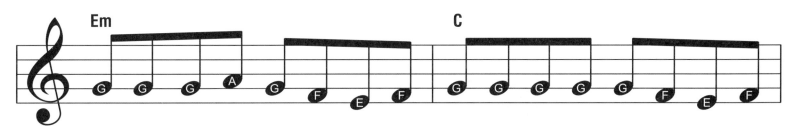

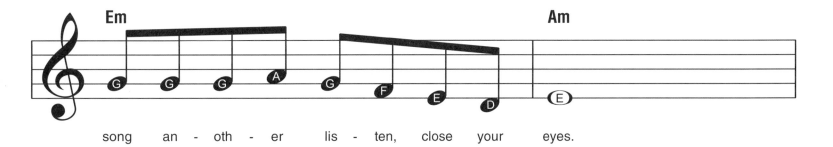

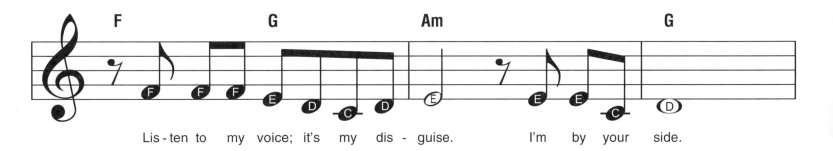

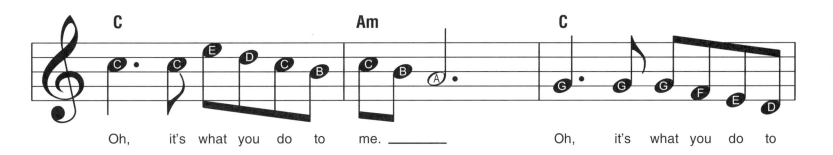

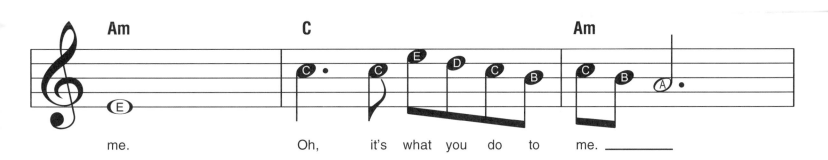

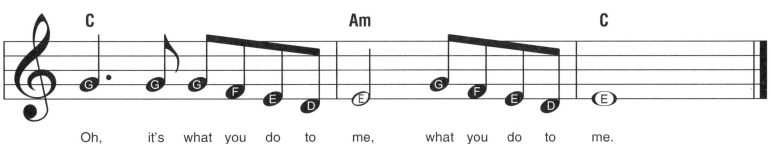

Ho Hey

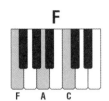
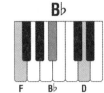
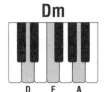
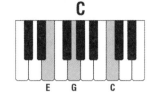

Words and Music by Jeremy Fraites
and Wesley Schultz

Brightly

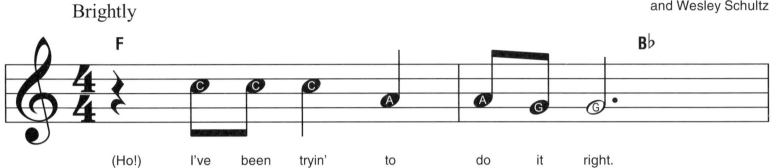

(Ho!) I've been tryin' to do it right.

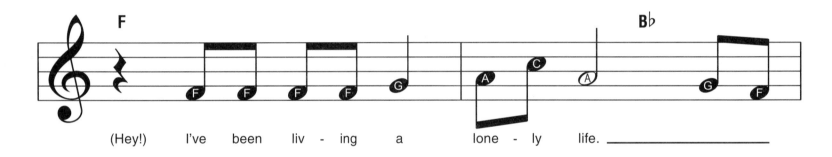

(Hey!) I've been liv - ing a lone - ly life. _____

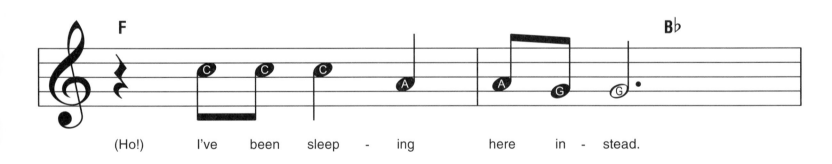

(Ho!) I've been sleep - ing here in - stead.

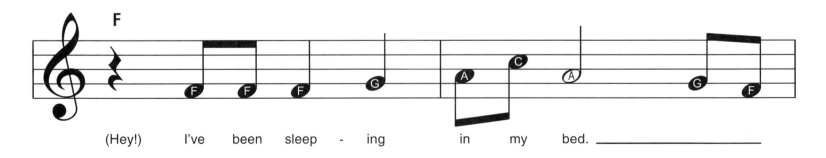

(Hey!) I've been sleep - ing in my bed. _____

43

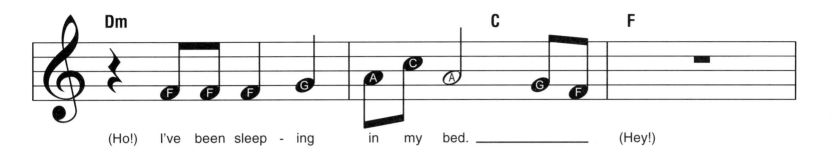

(Ho!) I've been sleep - ing   in my bed. _____ (Hey!)

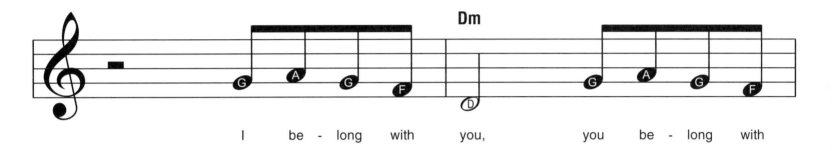

I   be - long with you,   you be - long with

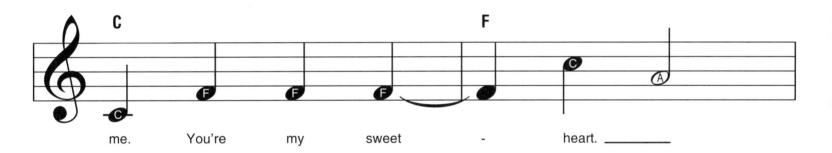

me.   You're   my   sweet   -   heart. _____

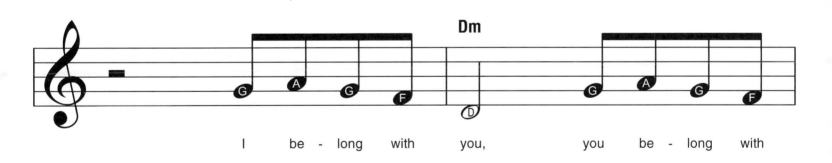

I   be - long with you,   you be - long with

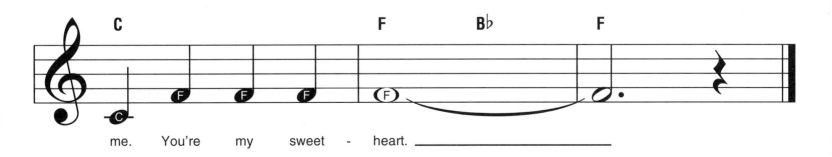

me.   You're   my   sweet - heart. _____

Home

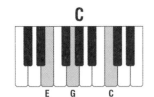
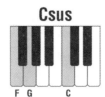
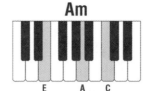
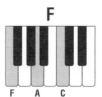
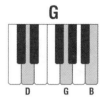

Words and Music by Greg Holden
and Drew Pearson

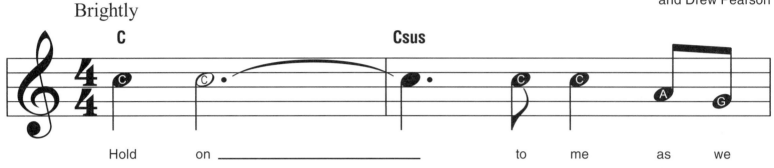

Hold on _____ to me as we

go,   (Instrumental)   as we roll down _____

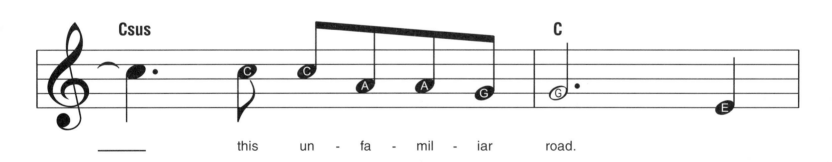

_____ this un - fa - mil - iar road.

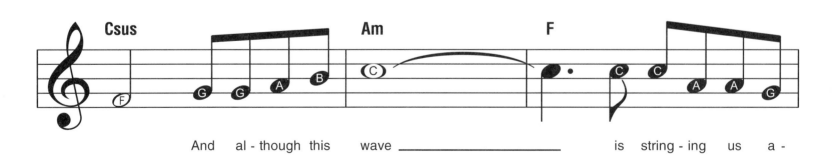

And al - though this wave _____ is string - ing us a-

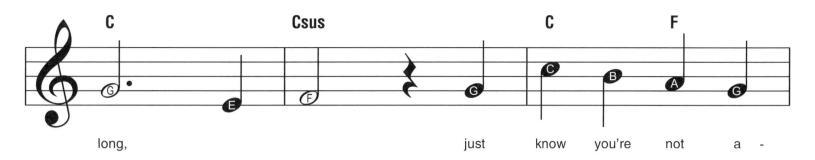

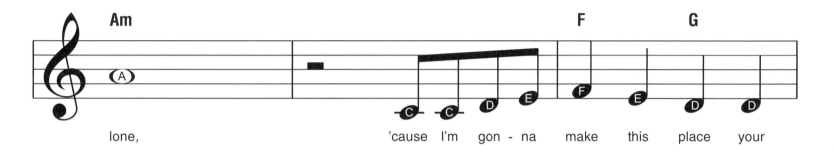

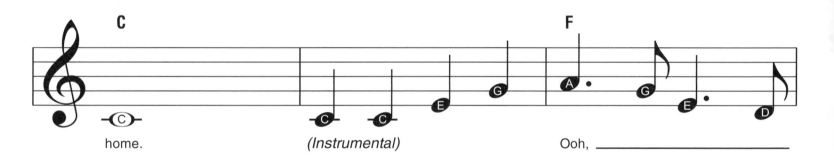

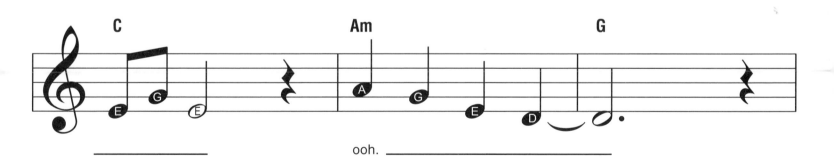

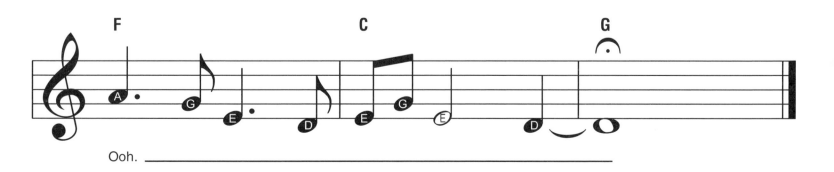

I Will Wait

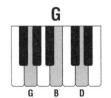 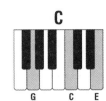 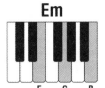 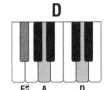 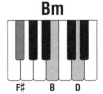

Words and Music by
Mumford & Sons

Moderately fast

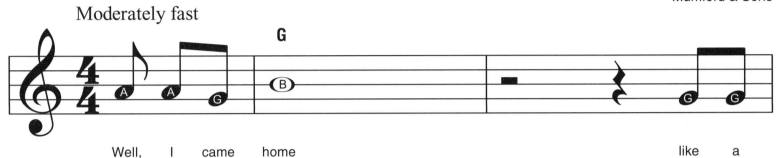

Well, I came home   like a

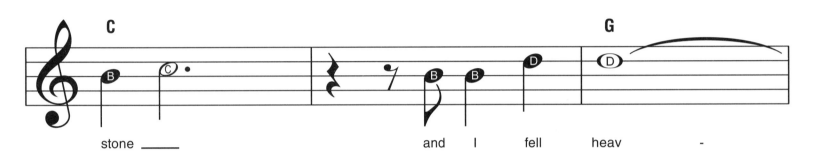

stone _____   and I fell heav -

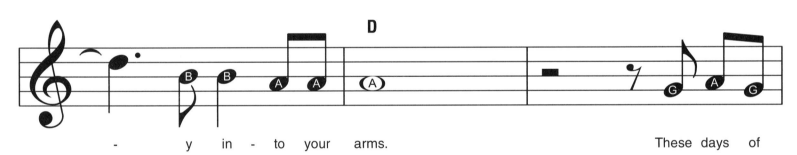

- y in - to your arms.   These days of

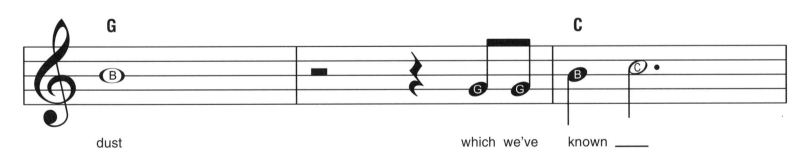

dust   which we've known _____

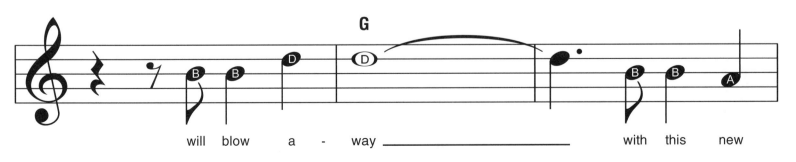

will blow a - way _____ with this new

I'm Not the Only One

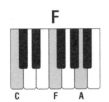
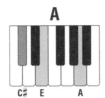

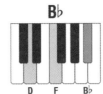
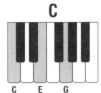

Words and Music by Sam Smith
and James Napier

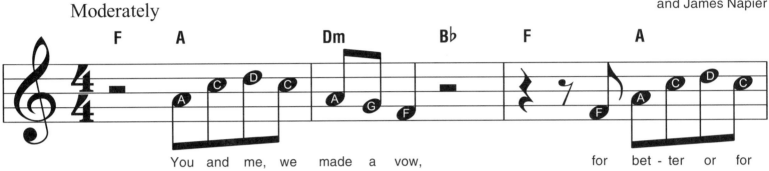

You and me, we made a vow, for bet - ter or for

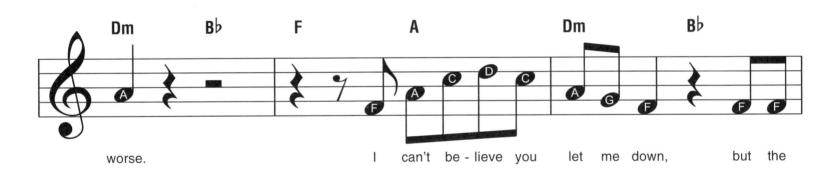

worse. I can't be - lieve you let me down, but the

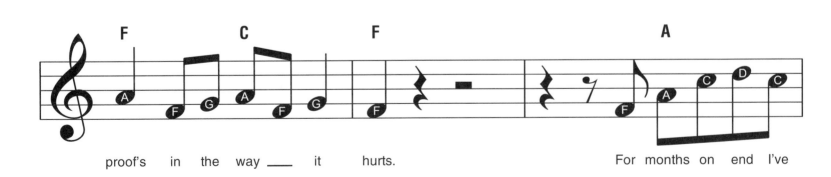

proof's in the way ___ it hurts. For months on end I've

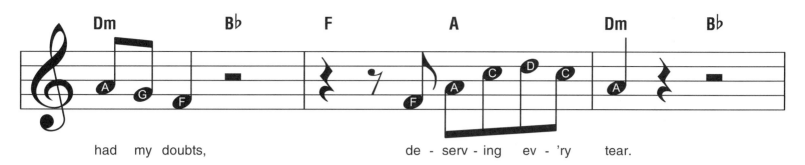

had my doubts, de - serv - ing ev - 'ry tear.

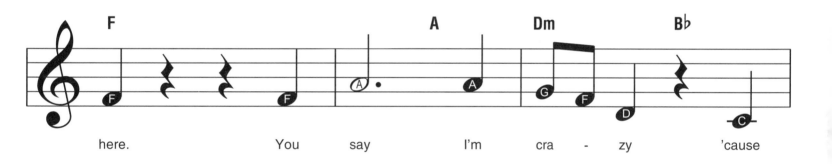

I wish this would be o - ver now, but I know that I still need you ___

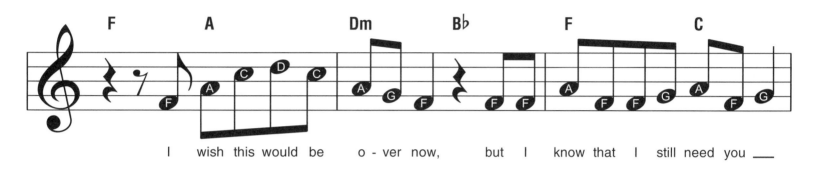

here. You say I'm cra - zy 'cause

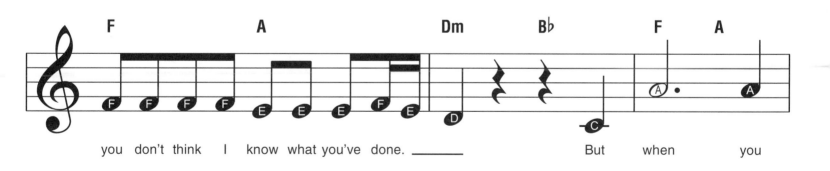

you don't think I know what you've done. _____ But when you

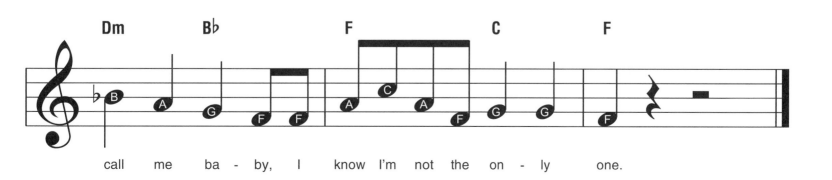

call me ba - by, I know I'm not the on - ly one.

I'm Yours

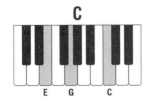
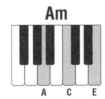
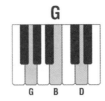
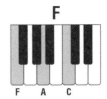

Words and Music by
Jason Mraz

Moderately fast Shuffle

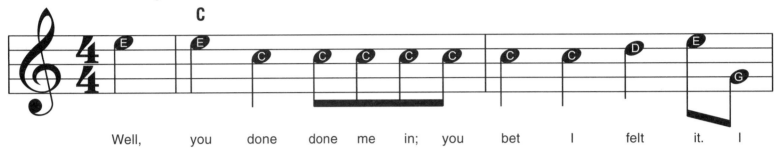

Well,   you   done   done   me   in;   you   bet   I   felt   it.   I

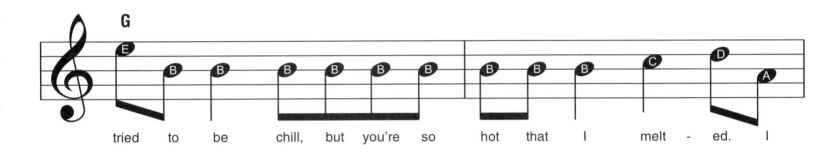

tried   to   be   chill,   but   you're   so   hot   that   I   melt - ed.   I

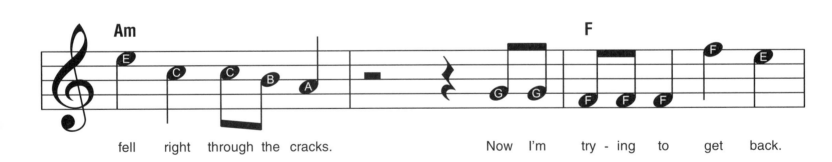

fell   right   through   the   cracks.   Now I'm   try - ing   to   get   back.

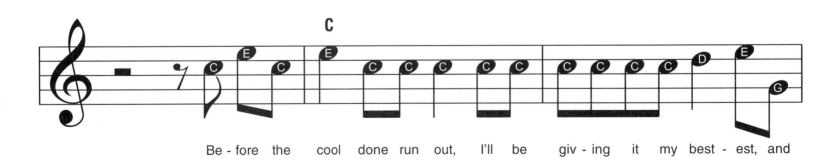

Be - fore   the   cool   done   run   out,   I'll   be   giv - ing   it   my   best - est,   and

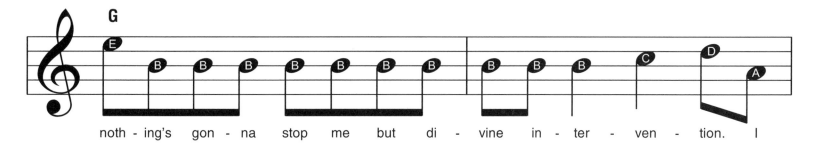

noth - ing's gon - na stop me but di - vine in - ter - ven - tion. I

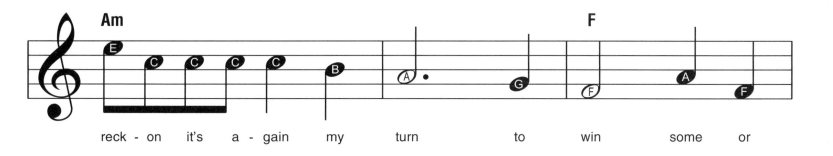

reck - on it's a - gain my turn to win some or

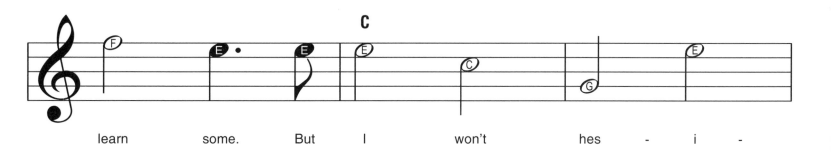

learn some. But I won't hes - i -

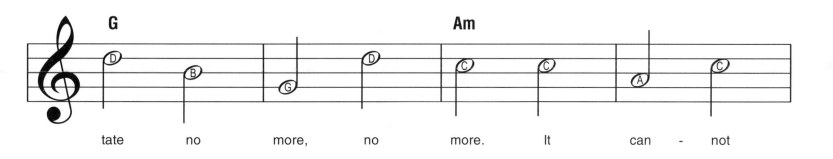

tate no more, no more. It can - not

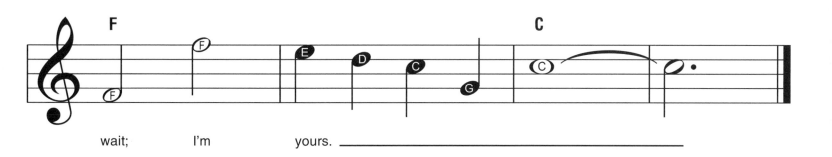

wait; I'm yours. _____

Jar of Hearts

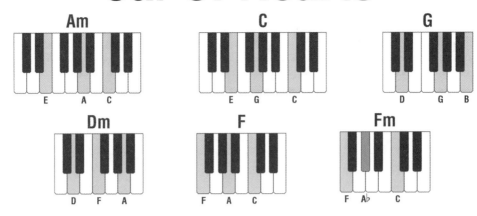

Words and Music by Barrett Yeretsian,
Christina Perri and Drew Lawrence

Moderate half-time feel

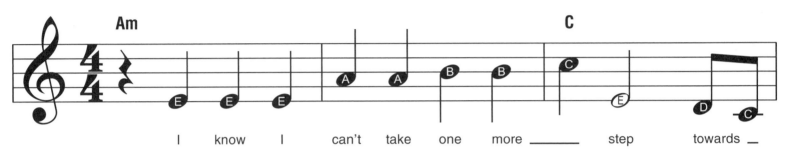

I know I can't take one more _____ step towards ___

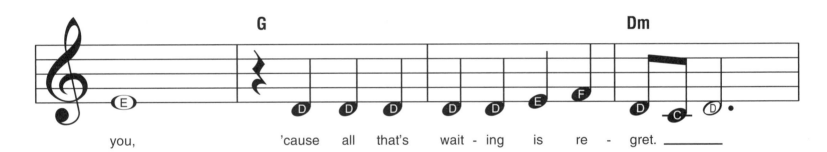

you, 'cause all that's wait-ing is re - gret. _____

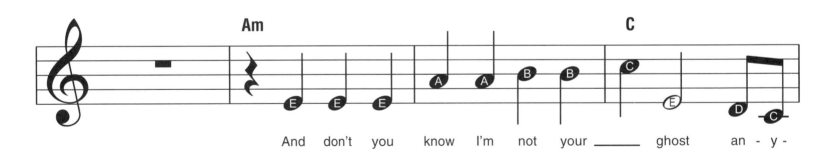

And don't you know I'm not your _____ ghost an - y-

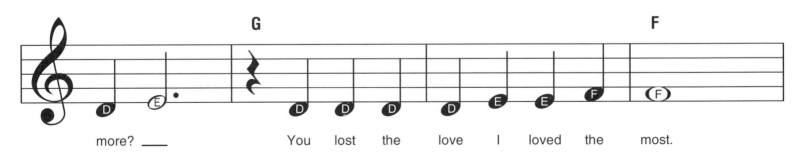

more? ___ You lost the love I loved the most.

Just Give Me a Reason

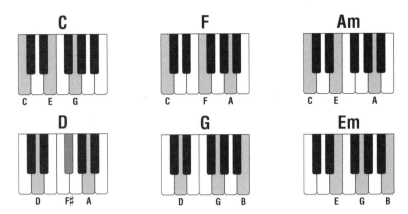

Words and Music by Alecia Moore,
Jeff Bhasker and Nate Ruess

Moderately

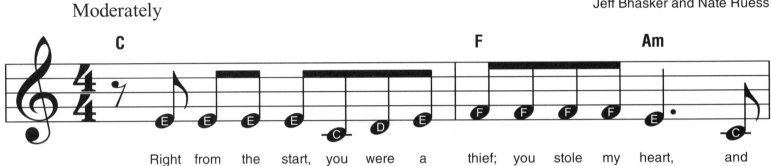

Right from the start, you were a thief; you stole my heart, and

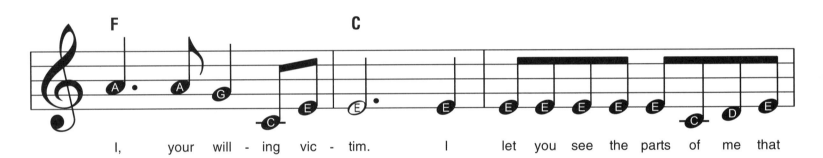

I, your will - ing vic - tim. I let you see the parts of me that

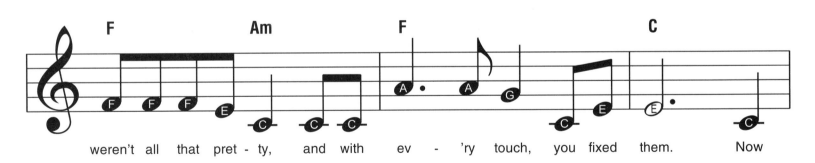

weren't all that pret - ty, and with ev - 'ry touch, you fixed them. Now

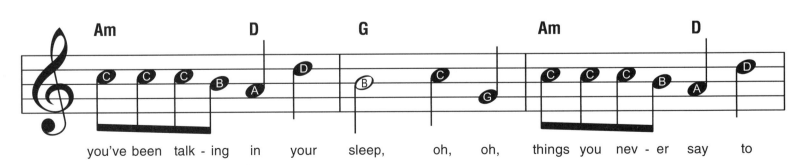

you've been talk - ing in your sleep, oh, oh, things you nev - er say to

Let Her Go

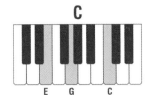
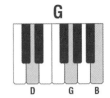
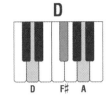
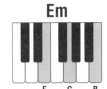
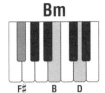

Words and Music by
Michael David Rosenberg

Moderately fast

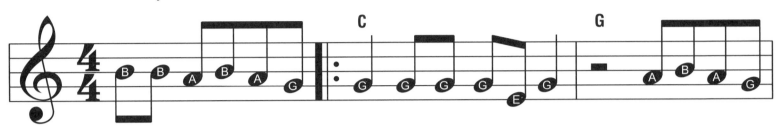

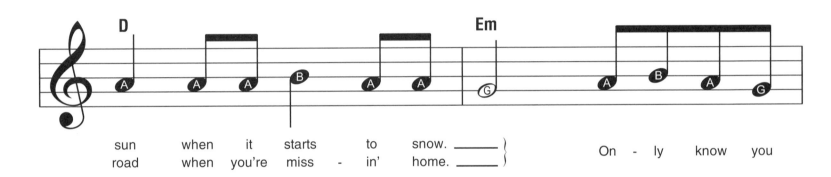

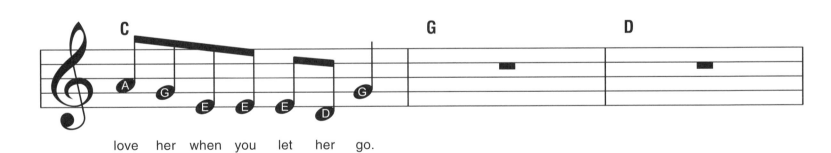

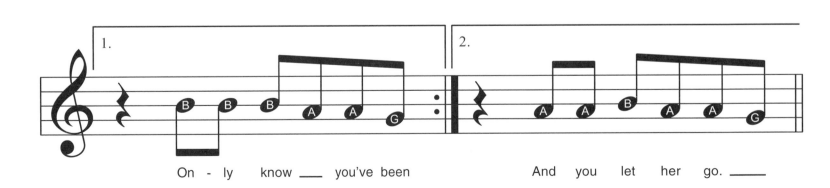

Let It Go

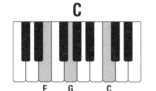 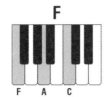 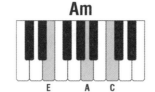 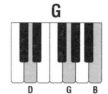 

Words and Music by James Bay
and Paul Barry

Moderately fast

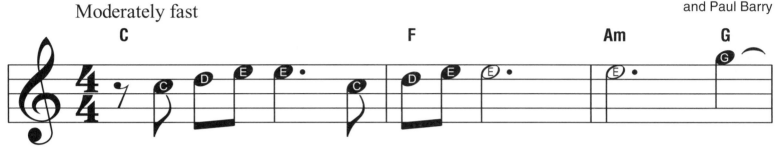

From walk - ing home and talk - ing loads, *(Instrumental)*

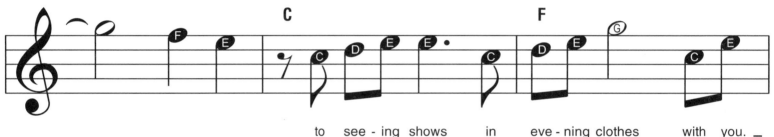

to see - ing shows in eve - ning clothes with you. _

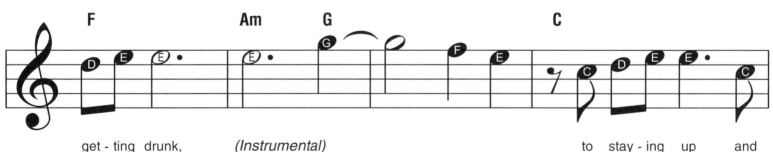

_____ *(Instrumental)* From nerv - ous touch and

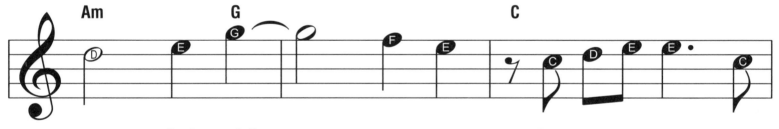

get - ting drunk, *(Instrumental)* to stay - ing up and

wak - ing up with you. _____ *(Instrumental)* But now we're

Let It Go
from FROZEN

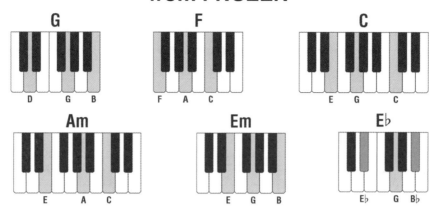

Music and Lyrics by Kristen Anderson-Lopez
and Robert Lopez

Flowing

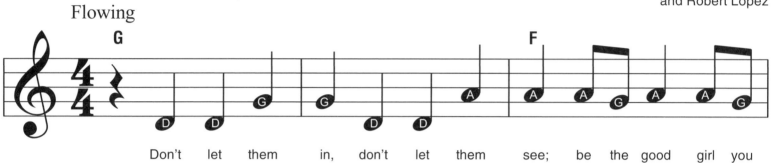

Don't let them in, don't let them see; be the good girl you

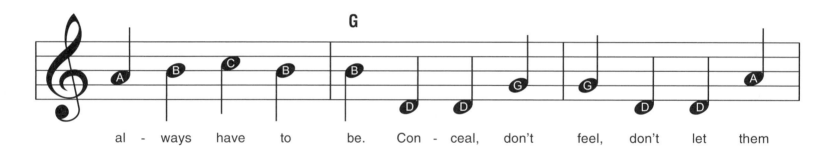

al - ways have to be. Con - ceal, don't feel, don't let them

know... Well, now they know. ____

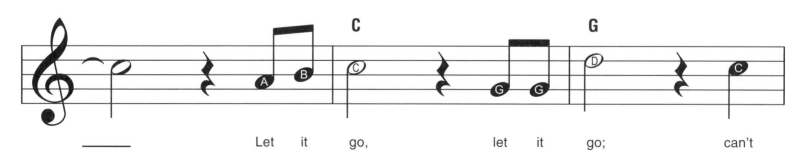

Let it go, let it go; can't

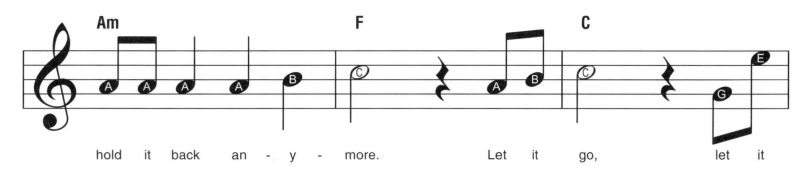

hold it back an - y - more. Let it go, let it

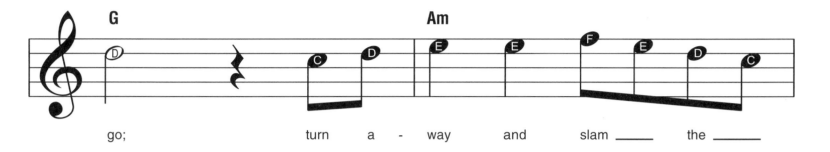

go; turn a - way and slam _____ the _____

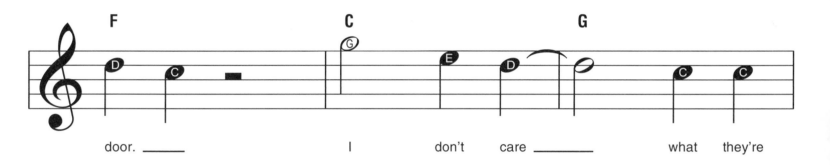

door. _____ I don't care _____ what they're

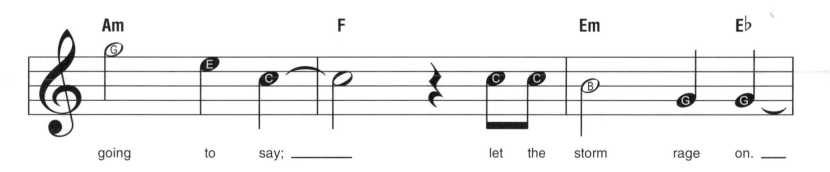

going to say; _____ let the storm rage on. ___

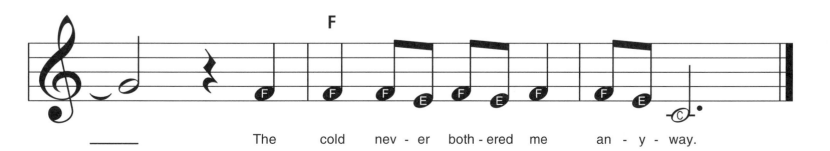

_____ The cold nev - er both - ered me an - y - way.

Little Talks

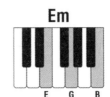 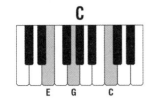 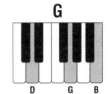 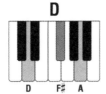

Words and Music by
Of Monsters And Men

Moderate half-time feel

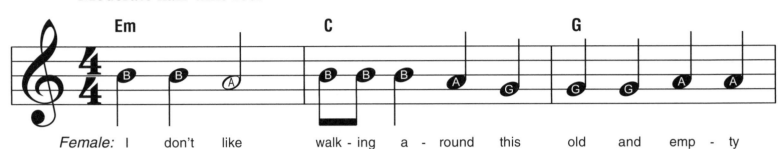

Female: I don't like walk - ing a - round this old and emp - ty

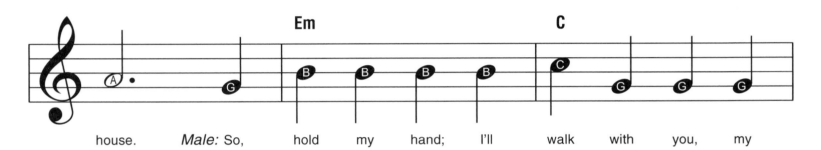

house. Male: So, hold my hand; I'll walk with you, my

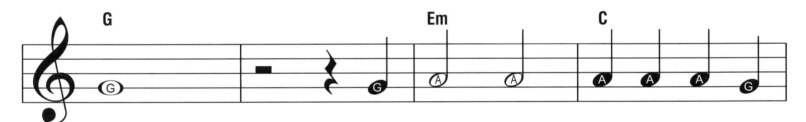

dear. Female: The stairs creak as you sleep; it's

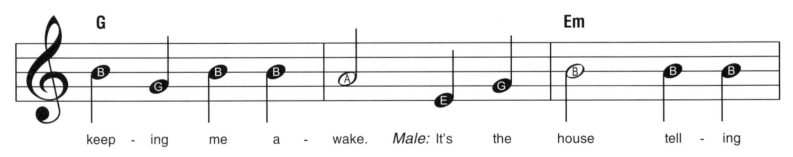

keep - ing me a - wake. Male: It's the house tell - ing

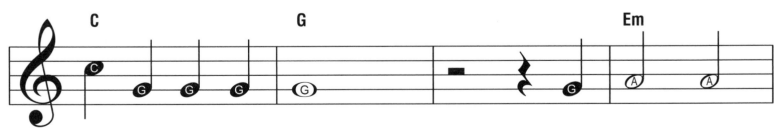

you to close your eyes. Female: And some days

63

Lost Boy

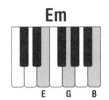
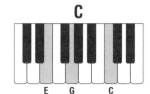
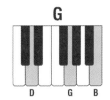

Words and Music by
Ruth Berhe

Moderately

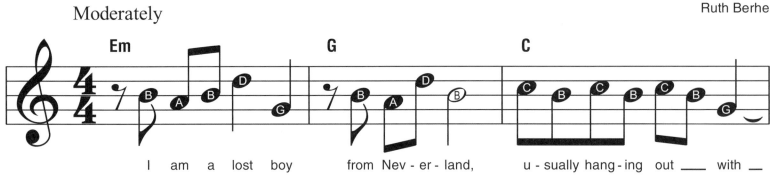

I am a lost boy from Nev - er - land, u - sually hang - ing out ___ with ___

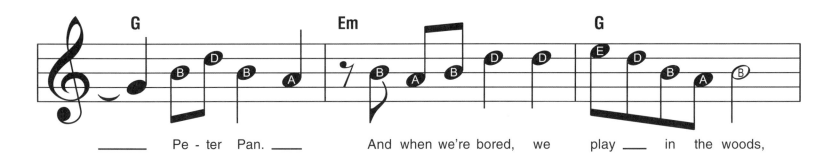

___ Pe - ter Pan. ___ And when we're bored, we play ___ in the woods,

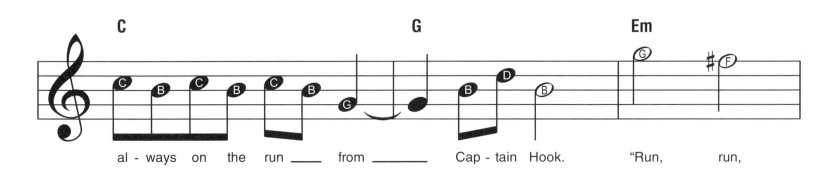

al - ways on the run ___ from ___ Cap - tain Hook. "Run, run,

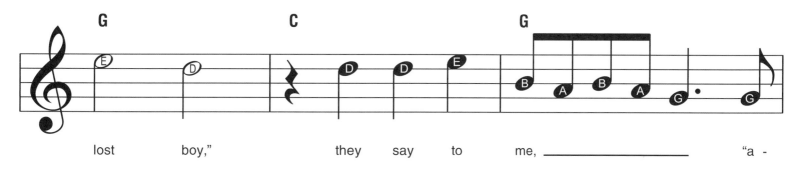

lost   boy,"   they   say   to   me, _____   "a -

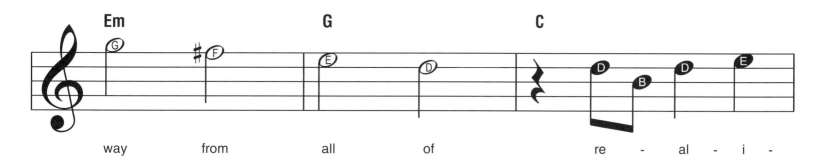

way   from   all   of   re - al - i -

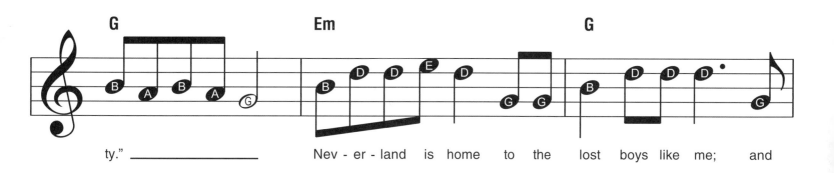

ty." _____   Nev - er - land is home to the lost boys like me;   and

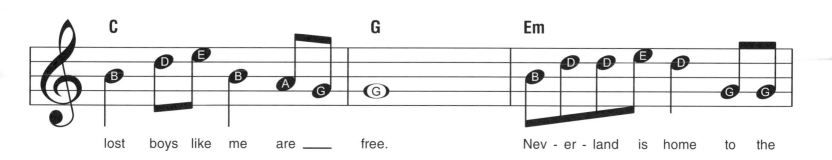

lost   boys   like   me   are ____ free.   Nev - er - land is home to the

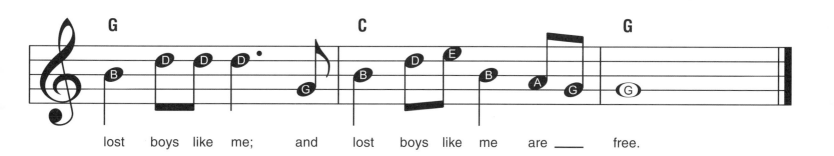

lost   boys   like   me;   and   lost   boys   like   me   are ____ free.

Love Yourself

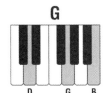
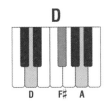
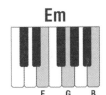
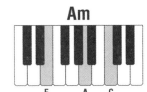
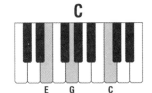

Words and Music by Justin Bieber,
Benjamin Levin and Ed Sheeran

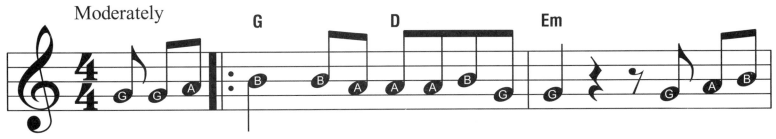

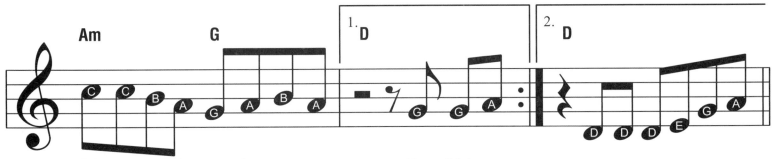

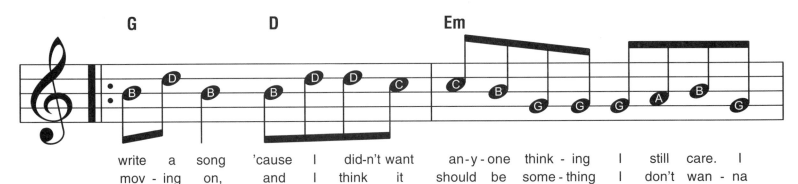

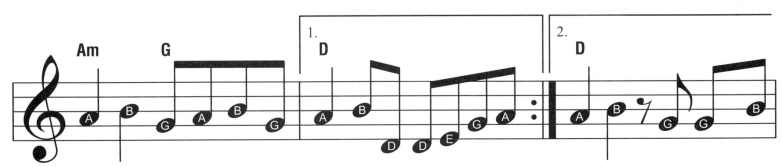

Mean

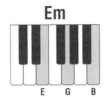
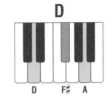
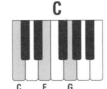
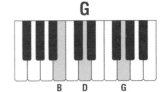

Words and Music by
Taylor Swift

Bright Country

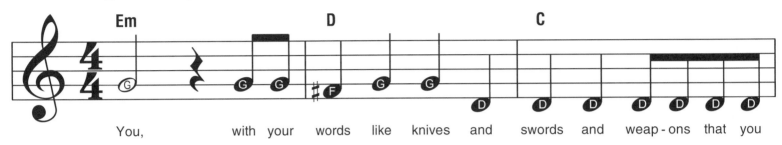

You,   with your words like knives and swords and weap-ons that you

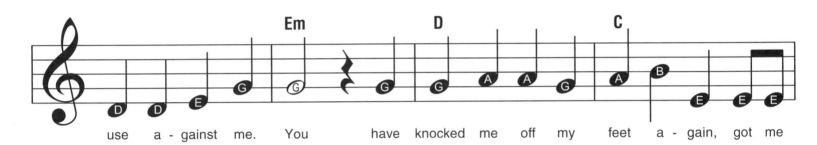

use a-gainst me. You   have knocked me off my feet a-gain, got me

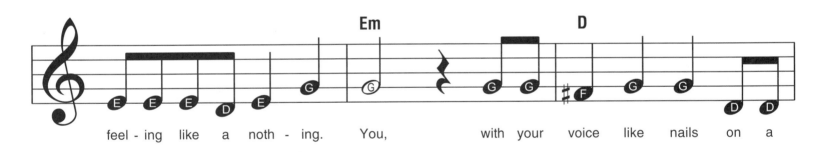

feel-ing like a noth-ing. You,   with your voice like nails on a

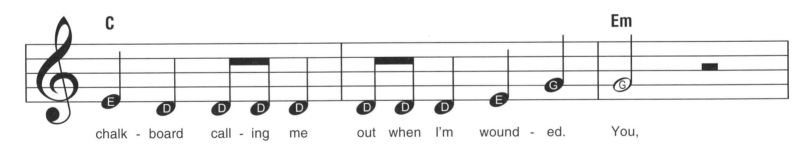

chalk-board call-ing me   out when I'm wound-ed. You,

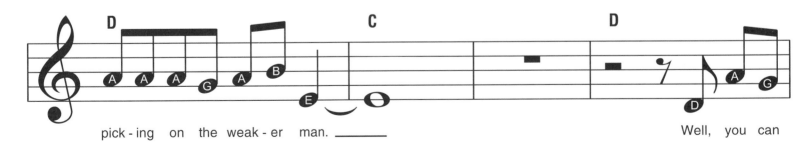

pick-ing on the weak-er man. _____   Well, you can

No One

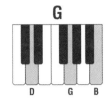
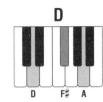
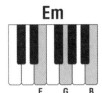
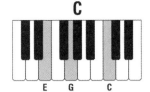

Words and Music by Alicia Keys,
Kerry Brothers, Jr. and George Harry

Moderately

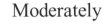
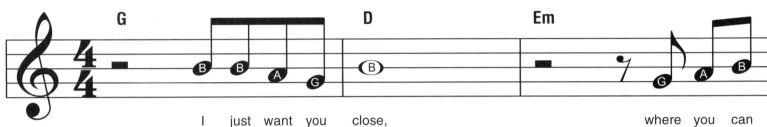

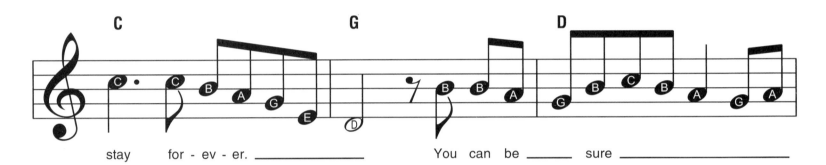

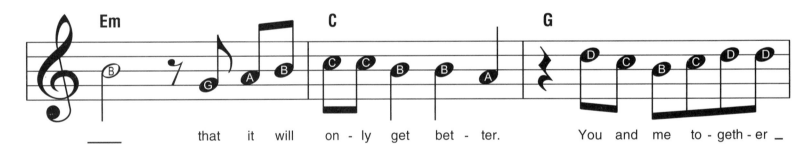

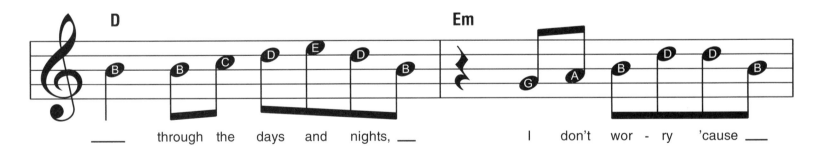

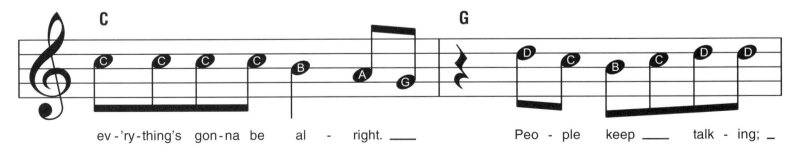

One Call Away

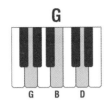
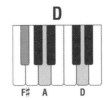
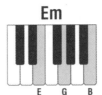
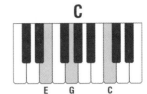

Words and Music by Charlie Puth,
Breyan Isaac, Matt Prime,
Justin Franks, Blake Anthony Carter
and Maureen McDonald

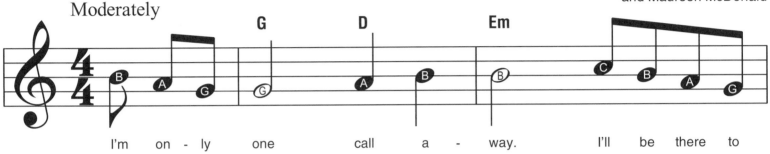

I'm on - ly one call a - way. I'll be there to

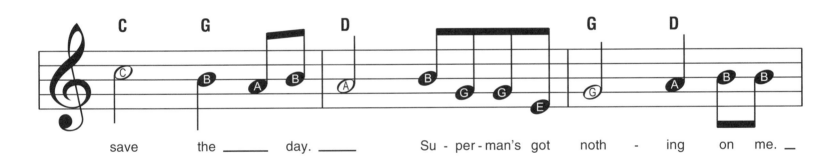

save the ____ day. ____ Su - per - man's got noth - ing on me. __

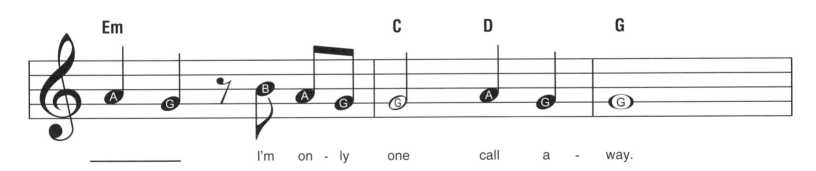

____ I'm on - ly one call a - way.

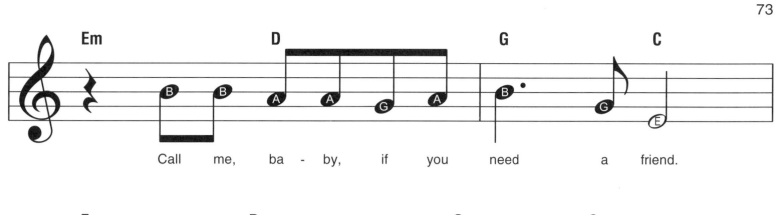

Call me, ba - by, if you need a friend.

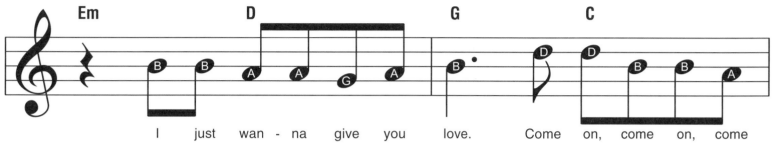

I just wan - na give you love. Come on, come on, come

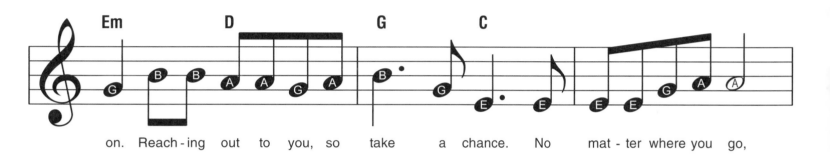

on. Reach-ing out to you, so take a chance. No mat - ter where you go,

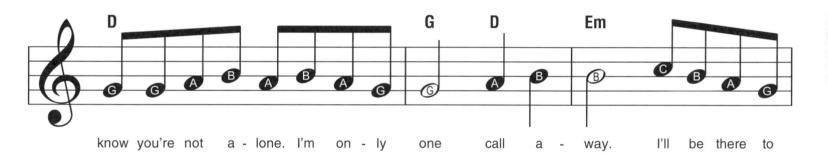

know you're not a - lone. I'm on - ly one call a - way. I'll be there to

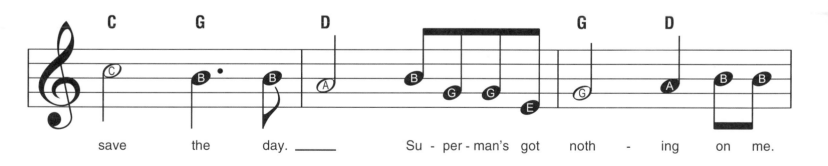

save the day. _____ Su - per-man's got noth - ing on me.

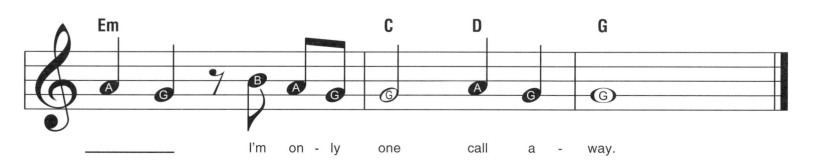

_____ I'm on - ly one call a - way.

100 Years

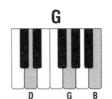 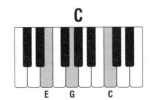 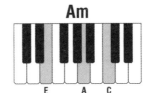 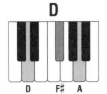 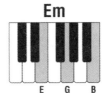

Words and Music by
John Ondrasik

Moderately fast

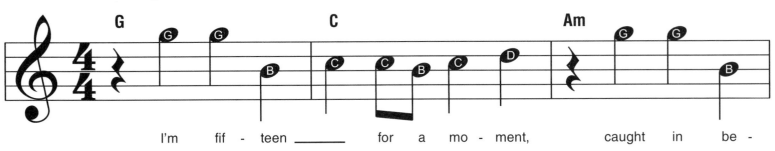

I'm fif - teen _____ for a mo - ment, caught in be -

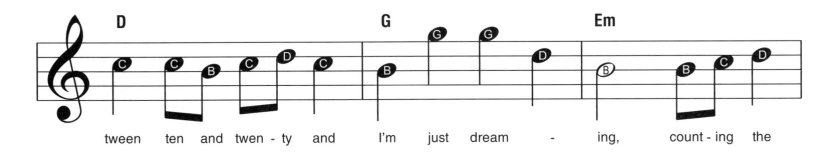

tween ten and twen - ty and I'm just dream - ing, count - ing the

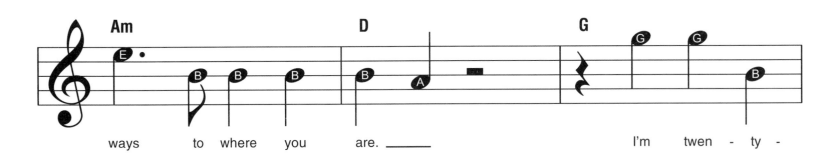

ways to where you are. _____ I'm twen - ty -

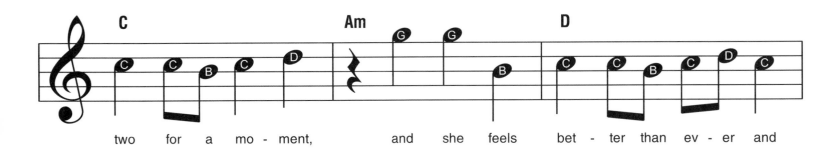

two for a mo - ment, and she feels bet - ter than ev - er and

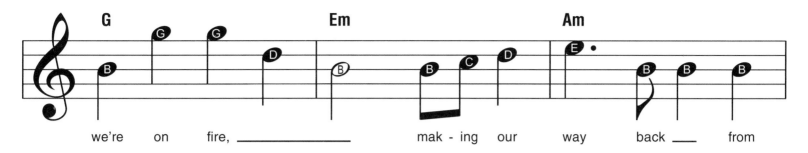

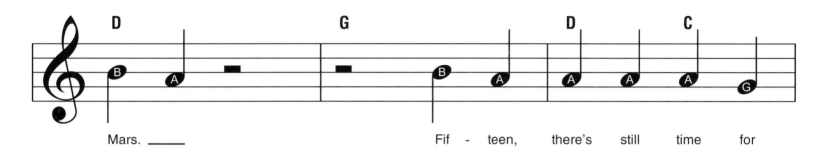

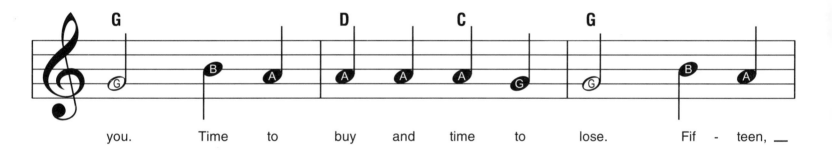

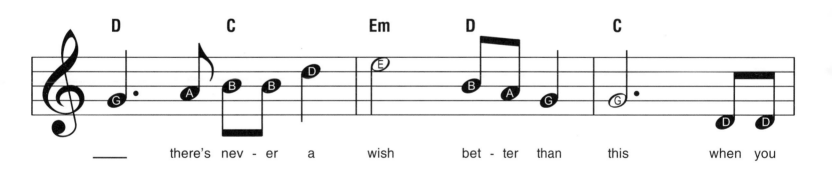

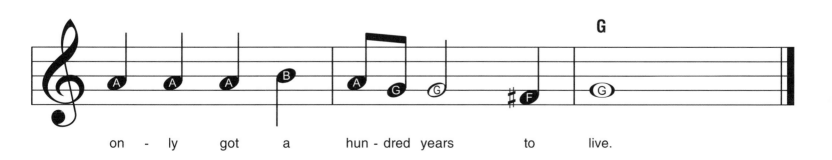

Poker Face

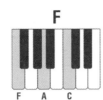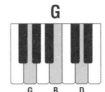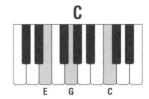

Words and Music by Stefani Germanotta
and RedOne

Moderately

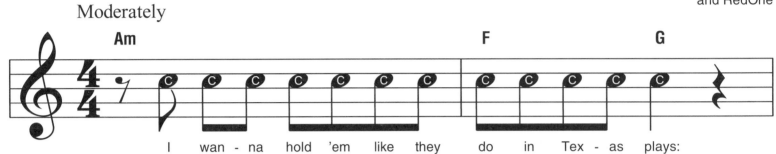

I wan-na hold 'em like they do in Tex-as plays:

fold 'em, let 'em hit me, raise it. Ba-by, stay with me.

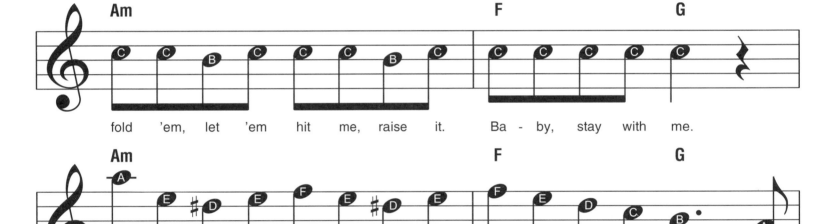

Luck and in-tu-i-tion play the cards with spades to start. And

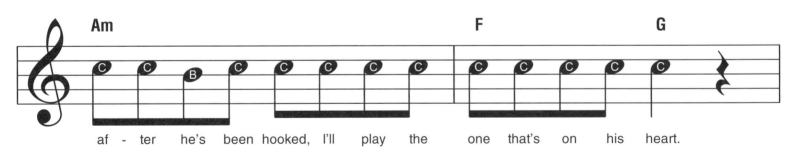

af-ter he's been hooked, I'll play the one that's on his heart.

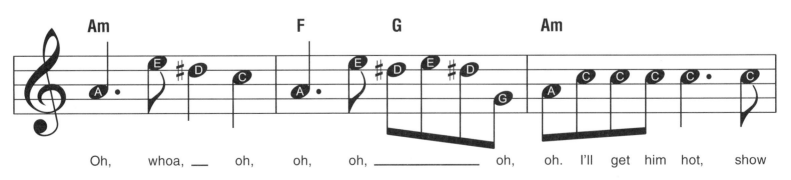

Oh, whoa, __ oh, oh, oh, _____ oh, oh. I'll get him hot, show

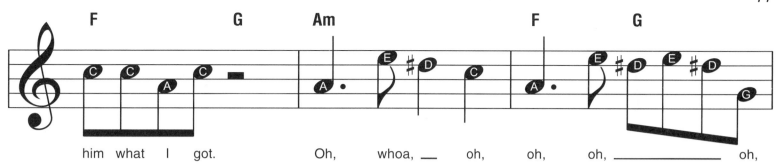

him what I got.　　Oh,　whoa, ___ oh,　oh,　oh, _____ oh,

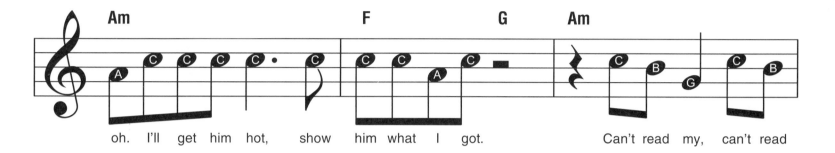

oh.　I'll get him hot,　show　him what I got.　　Can't read my,　can't read

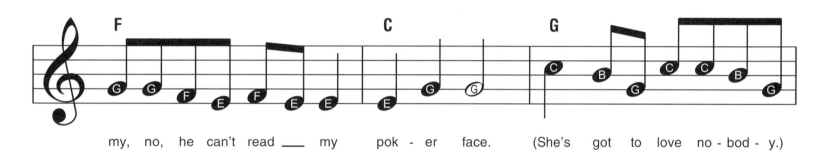

my, no, he can't read ___ my　pok - er　face.　(She's got to love no - bod - y.)

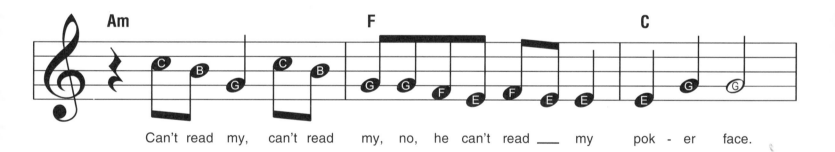

Can't read my,　can't read　my, no, he can't read ___ my　pok - er　face.

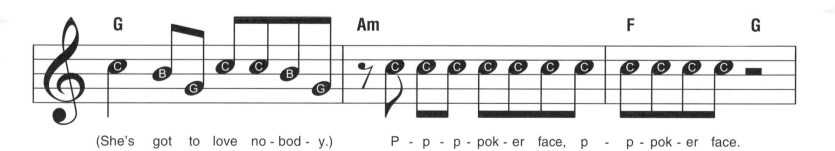

(She's got to love no - bod - y.)　P - p - p - pok - er face, p - p - pok - er face.

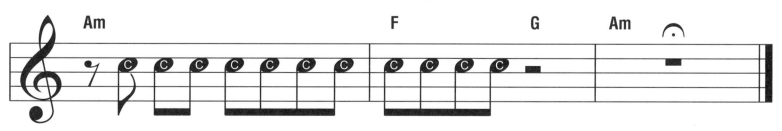

P - p - p - pok - er face, p - p - pok - er face.

Renegades

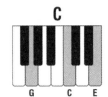
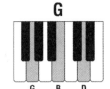
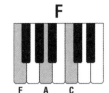

Words and Music by Alexander Junior Grant,
Adam Levin, Casey Harris,
Noah Feldshuh and Sam Harris

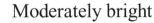

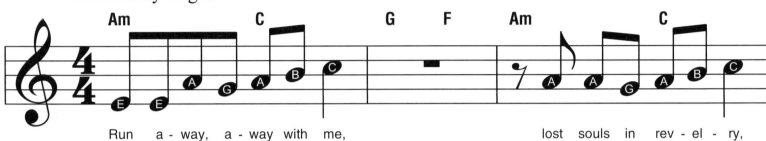

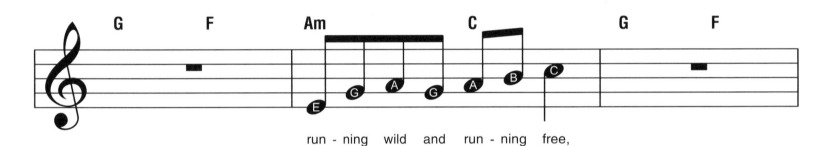

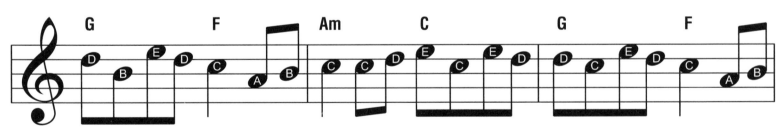

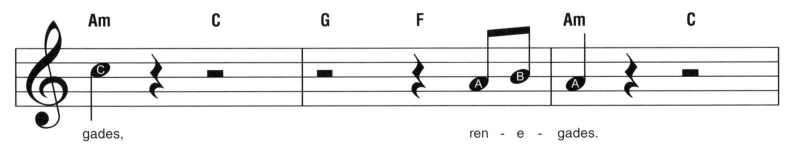

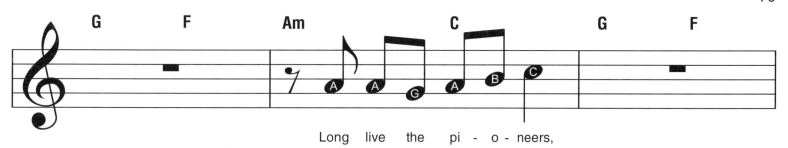

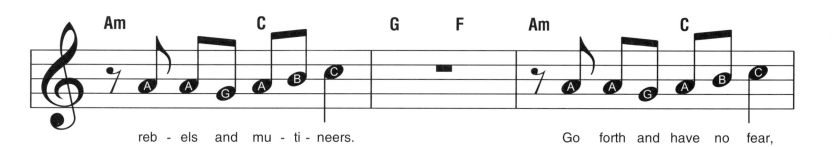

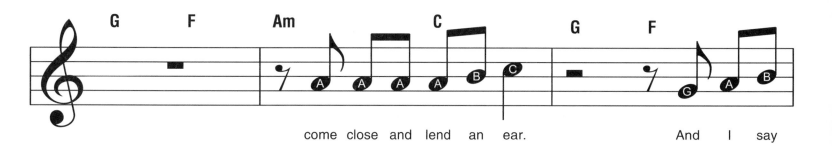

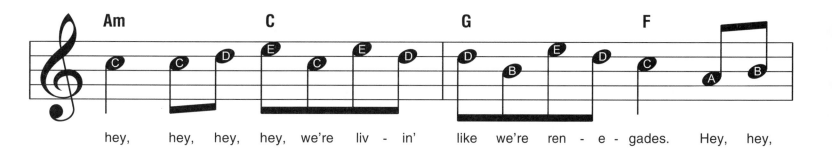

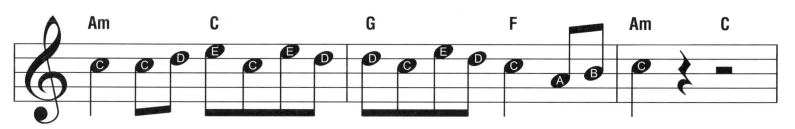

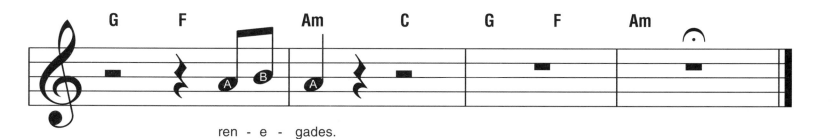

Riptide

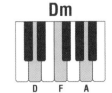
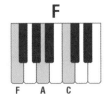
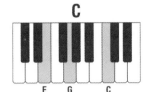

Words and Music by
Vance Joy

Moderately

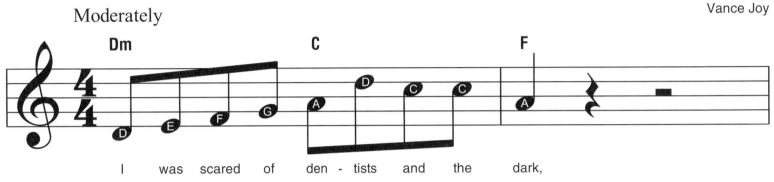

I was scared of den - tists and the dark,

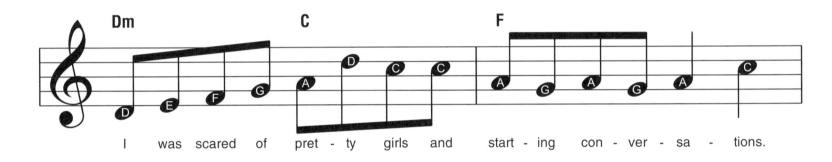

I was scared of pret - ty girls and start - ing con - ver - sa - tions.

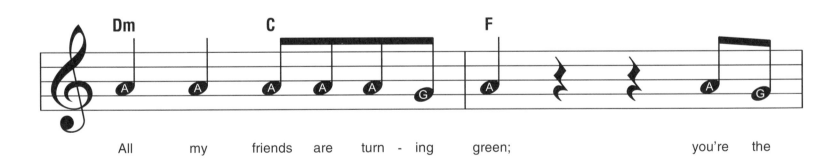

All my friends are turn - ing green; you're the

ma - gi - cian's as - sist - ant in their dream. _____ Ah ooh. _____

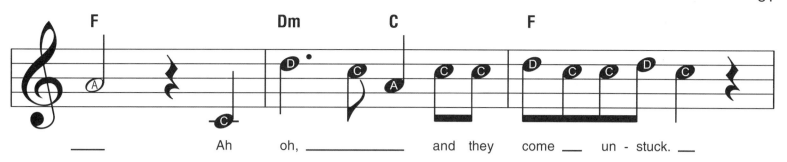

Ah oh, _____ and they come ___ un - stuck. ___

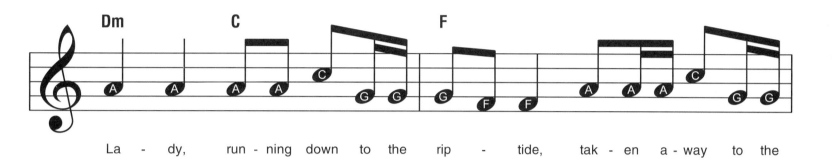

La - dy, run - ning down to the rip - tide, tak - en a - way to the

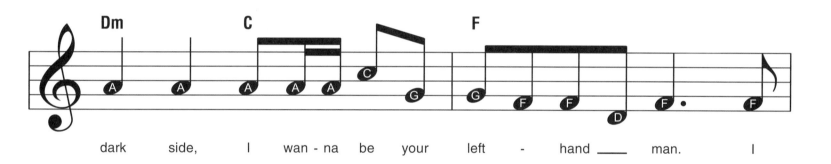

dark side, I wan - na be your left - hand ___ man. I

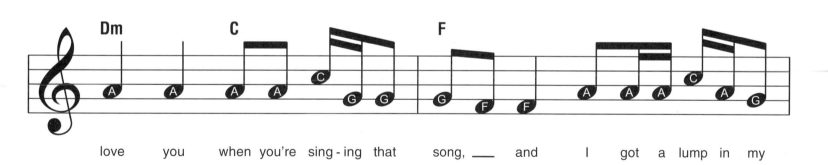

love you when you're sing - ing that song, ___ and I got a lump in my

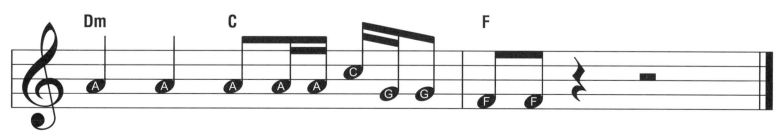

throat 'cause you're gon - na sing the words _____ wrong.

Roar

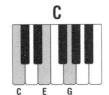 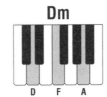 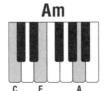 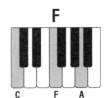

Words and Music by Katy Perry,
Lukasz Gottwald, Max Martin,
Bonnie McKee and Henry Walter

Quickly

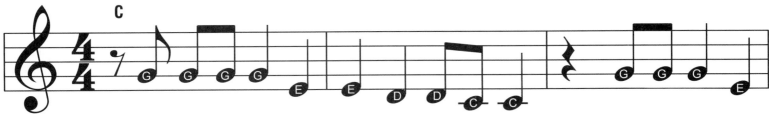

I used to bite my tongue and hold my breath, scared to rock the
I guess that I for-got I had a choice. I let you push me

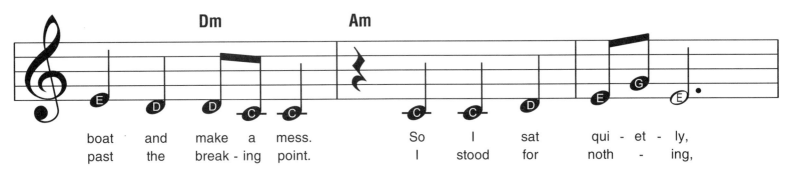

boat and make a mess. So I sat qui-et-ly,
past the break-ing point. I stood for noth-ing,

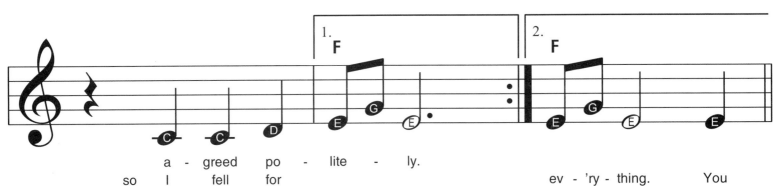

a-greed po-lite-ly.
so I fell for ev-'ry-thing. You

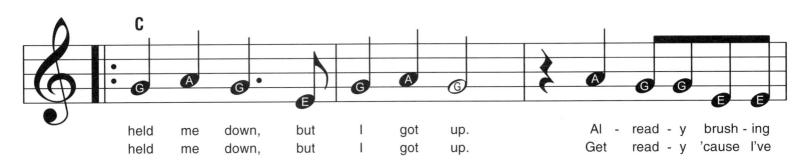

held me down, but I got up. Al-read-y brush-ing
held me down, but I got up. Get read-y 'cause I've

83

Rolling in the Deep

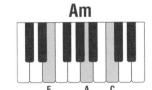
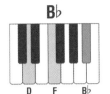
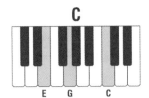
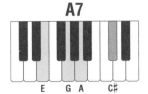
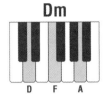

Words and Music by Adele Adkins
and Paul Epworth

Soulfully

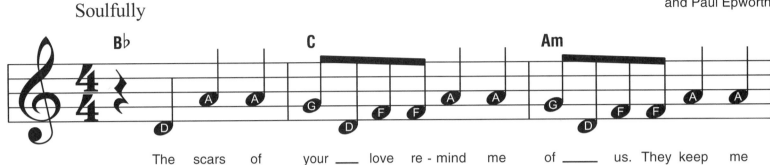

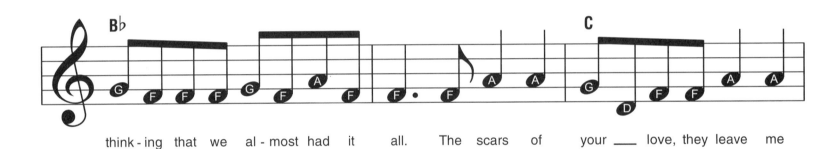

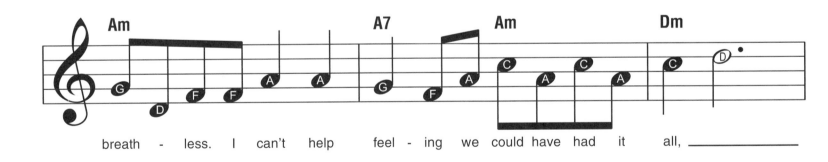

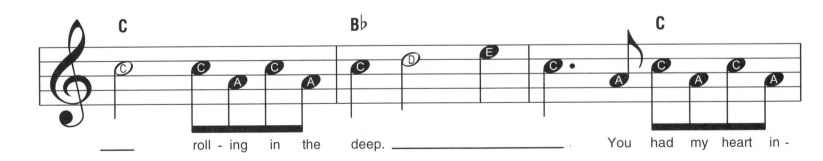

Royals

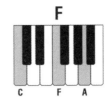
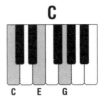
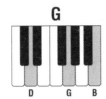

Words and Music by Ella Yelich-O'Connor
and Joel Little

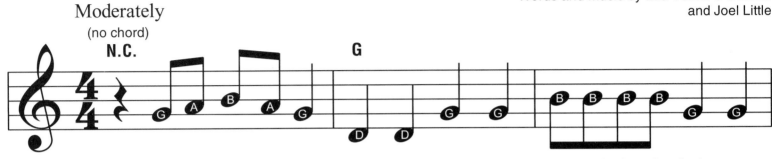

Moderately
(no chord)

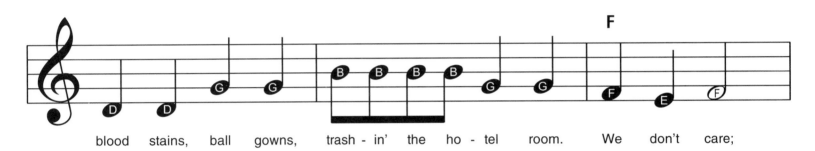

Ev - 'ry song's __ like: gold teeth, Grey Goose, trip-pin' in the bath-room,

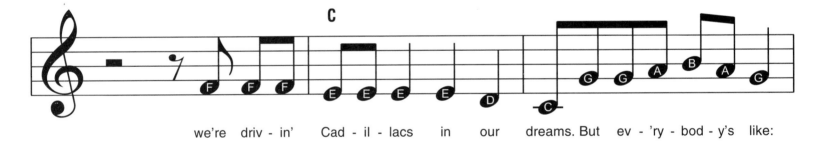

blood stains, ball gowns, trash - in' the ho - tel room. We don't care;

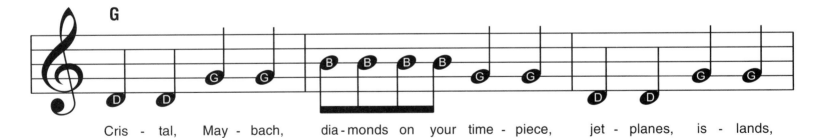

we're driv - in' Cad - il - lacs in our dreams. But ev - 'ry - bod - y's like:

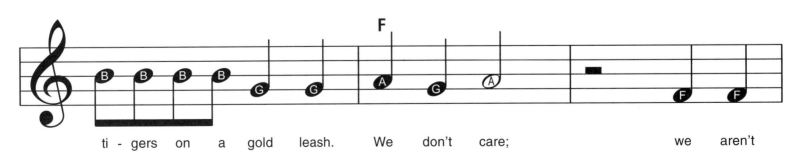

Cris - tal, May - bach, dia - monds on your time - piece, jet - planes, is - lands,

ti - gers on a gold leash. We don't care; we aren't

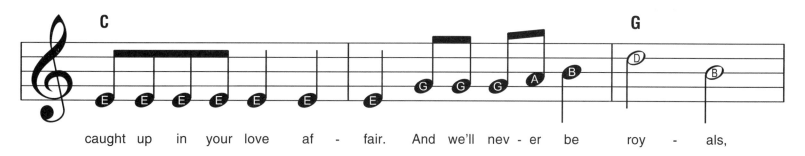

caught up in your love af - fair. And we'll nev - er be roy - als,

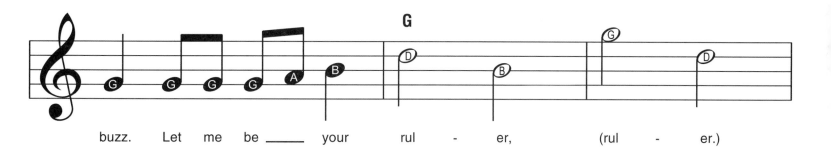

(roy - als.) It don't run in our ____ blood. That kind of

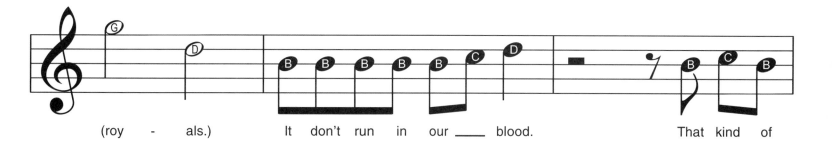

luxe just ain't for us. We crave a dif - f'rent kind of

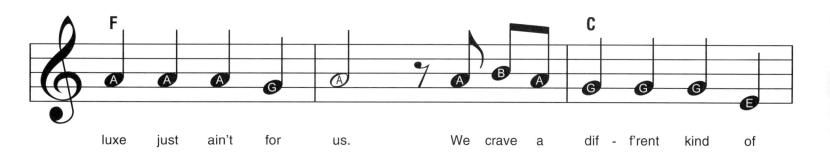

buzz. Let me be ____ your rul - er, (rul - er.)

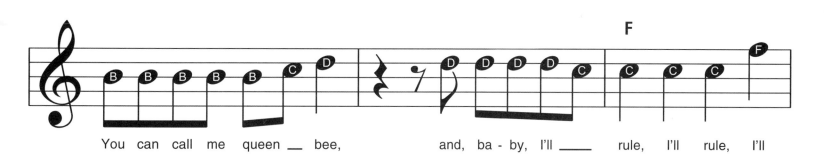

You can call me queen __ bee, and, ba - by, I'll ____ rule, I'll rule, I'll

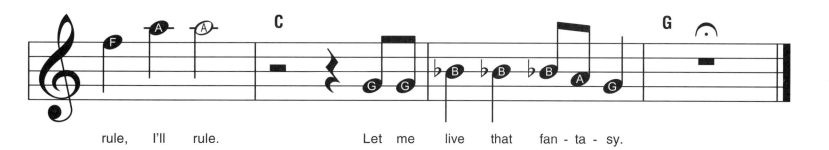

rule, I'll rule. Let me live that fan - ta - sy.

Say Something

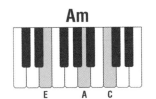
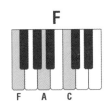
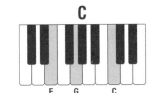
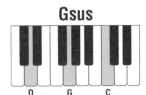
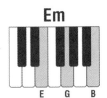

Words and Music by Ian Axel,
Chad Vaccarino and Mike Campbell

Gently

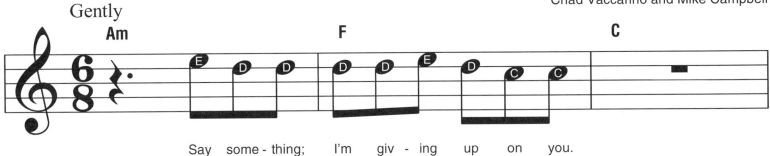

Say some-thing; I'm giv-ing up on you.

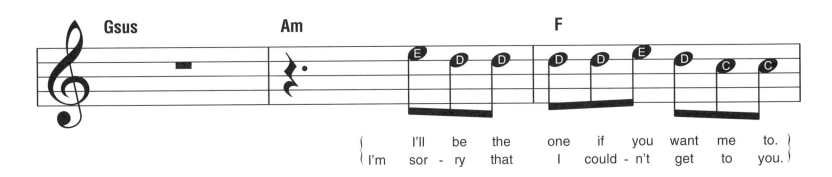

I'll be the one if you want me to.
I'm sor-ry that I could-n't get to you.

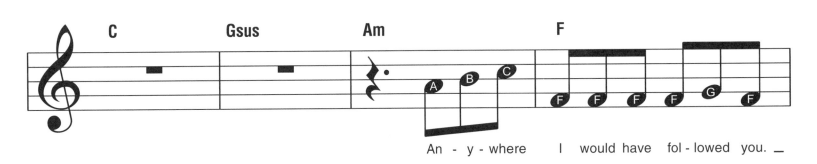

An-y-where I would have fol-lowed you.

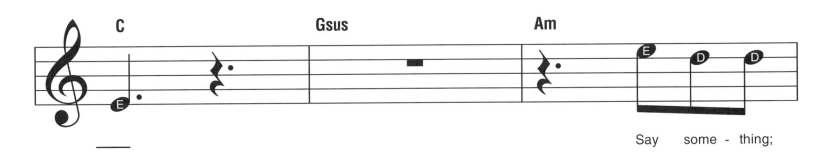

Say some-thing;

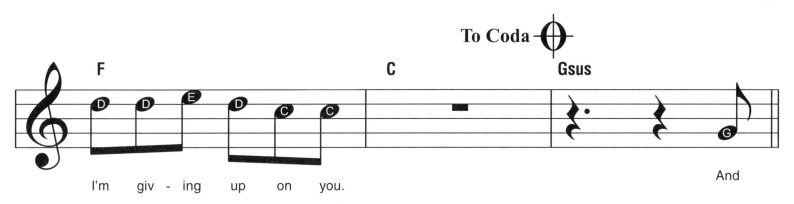

I'm giv - ing up on you.
And

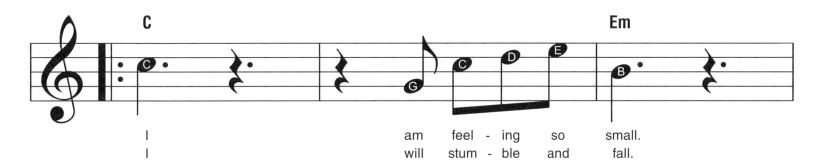

I
I
am feel - ing so small.
will stum - ble and fall.

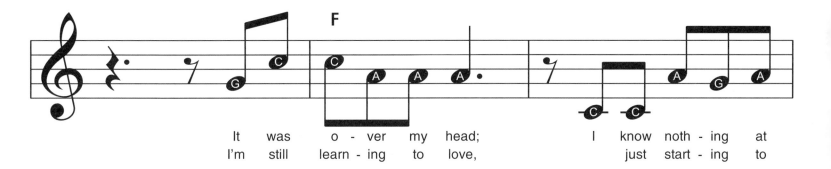

It was o - ver my head;
I'm still learn - ing to love,
I know noth - ing at
just start - ing to

all.
crawl.
And

D.C. al Coda
(Return to beginning,
play to ⊕ and skip to Coda)

CODA

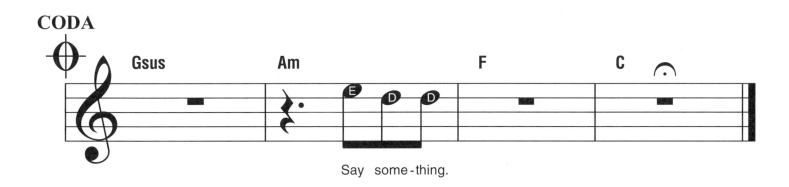

Say some - thing.

See You Again

from FURIOUS 7

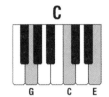
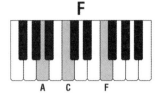

Words and Music by Cameron Thomaz,
Charlie Puth, Justin Franks
and Andrew Cedar

Moderately

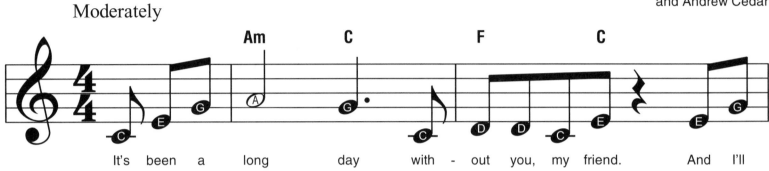

It's been a long day with-out you, my friend. And I'll

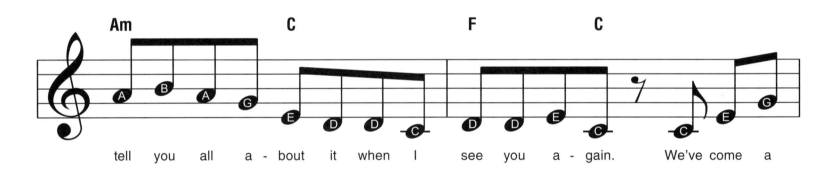

tell you all a-bout it when I see you a-gain. We've come a

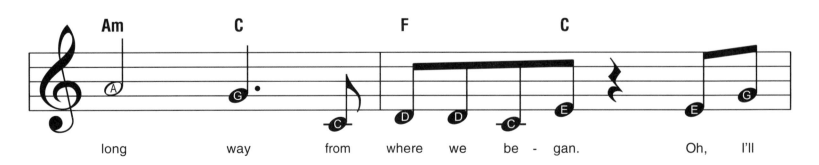

long way from where we be-gan. Oh, I'll

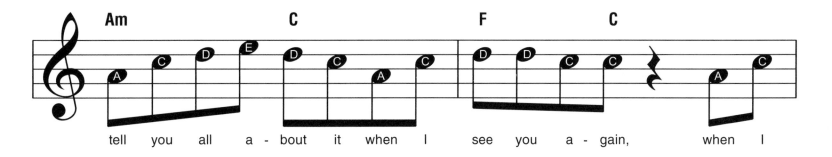

tell you all a - bout it when I see you a - gain, when I

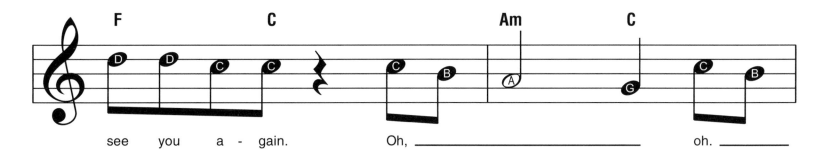

see you a - gain. Oh, _____ oh. _____

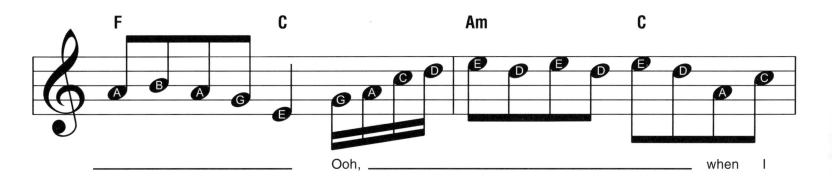

_____ Ooh, _____ when I

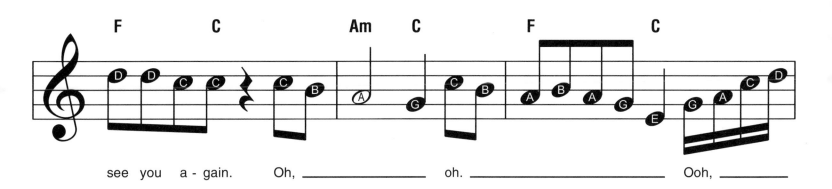

see you a - gain. Oh, _____ oh. _____ Ooh, _____

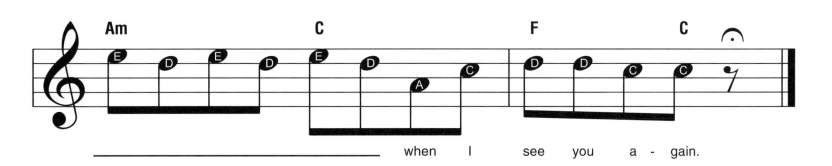

_____ when I see you a - gain.

7 Years

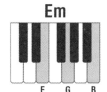 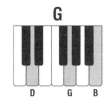 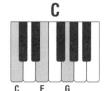 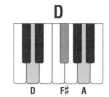

Words and Music by Lukas Forchhammer,
Morten Ristorp, Stefan Forrest,
David Labrel, Christopher Brown
and Morten Pilegaard

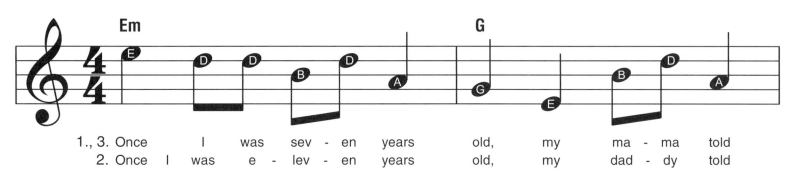

1., 3. Once I was sev - en years old, my ma - ma told
2. Once I was e - lev - en years old, my dad - dy told

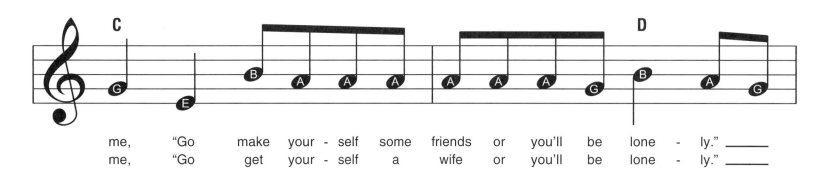

me, "Go make your - self some friends or you'll be lone - ly." ____
me, "Go get your - self a wife or you'll be lone - ly." ____

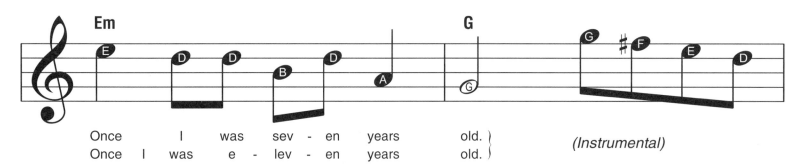

Once I was sev - en years old.
Once I was e - lev - en years old.

(Instrumental)

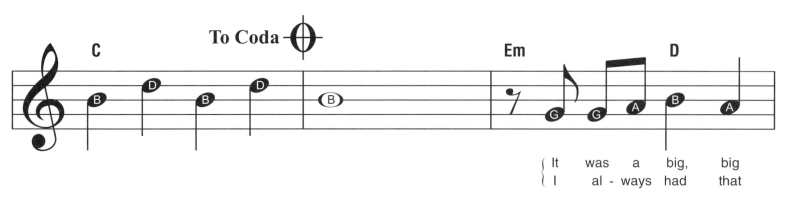

It was a big, big
I al - ways had that

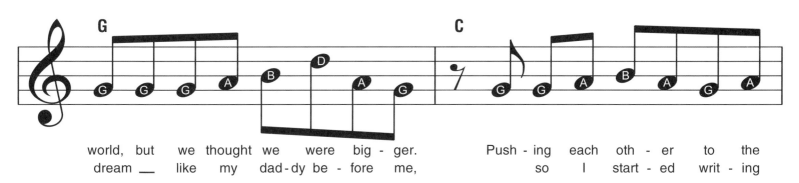

world, but   we thought we were big - ger.   Push - ing each oth - er to the
dream __ like my dad - dy be - fore me,   so   I   start - ed   writ - ing

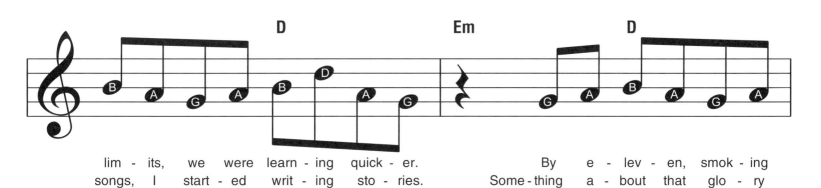

lim - its,   we were learn - ing quick - er.   By   e - lev - en, smok - ing
songs, I   start - ed writ - ing sto - ries.   Some - thing a - bout that glo - ry

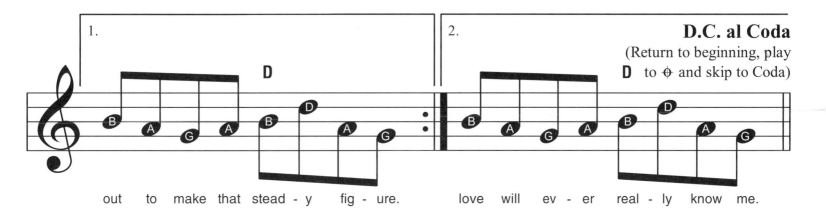

herb   and drink - ing burn - ing li - quor.   Nev - er rich, so we were
just   al - ways seemed to bore me,   'cause on - ly those I real - ly

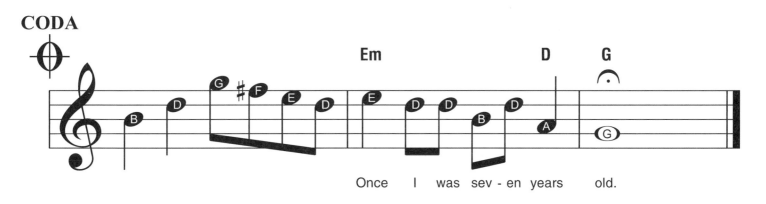

out   to make that stead - y   fig - ure.   love will ev - er real - ly know me.

Once   I   was sev - en years   old.

Shake It Off

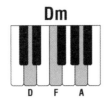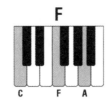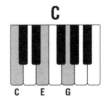

Words and Music by Taylor Swift,
Max Martin and Shellback

Moderately fast

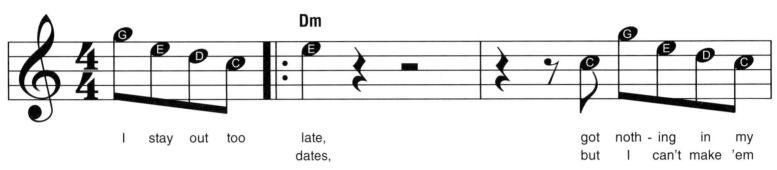

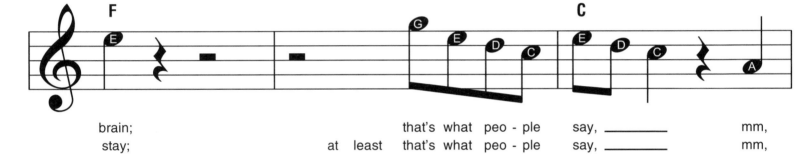

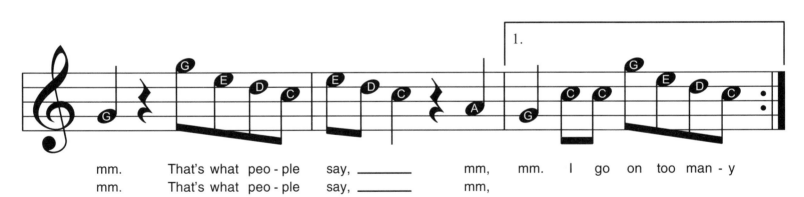

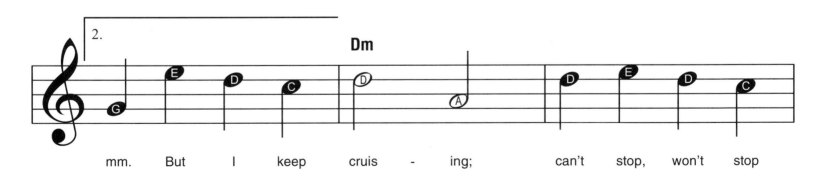

She Will Be Loved

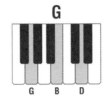
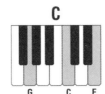
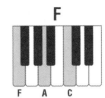

Words and Music by Adam Levine
and James Valentine

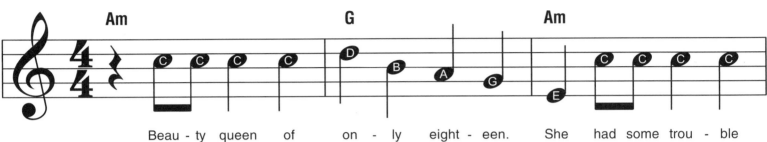

Beau - ty queen of on - ly eight - een. She had some trou - ble

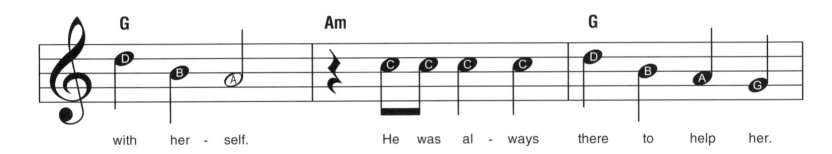

with her - self. He was al - ways there to help her.

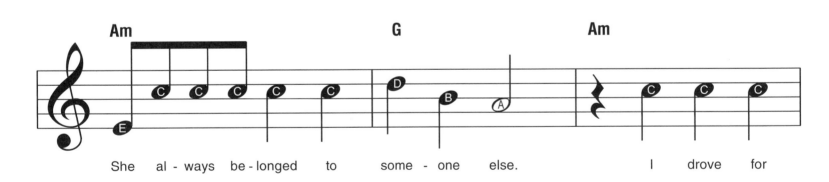

She al - ways be - longed to some - one else. I drove for

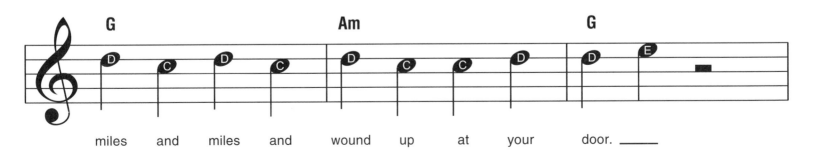

miles and miles and wound up at your door. _____

A Sky Full of Stars

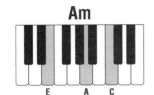
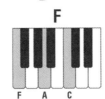
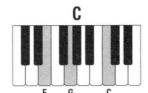
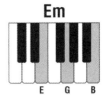

Words and Music by Guy Berryman,
Jon Buckland, Will Champion,
Chris Martin and Tim Bergling

Moderately fast

'Cause you're a sky, _____ 'cause you're a sky full of

stars. I'm gon-na give you my

heart. 'Cause you're a

sky, _____ 'cause you're a sky full of stars.

'Cause you light up the path.

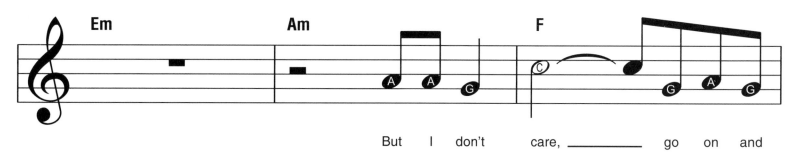

But I don't care, _____ go on and

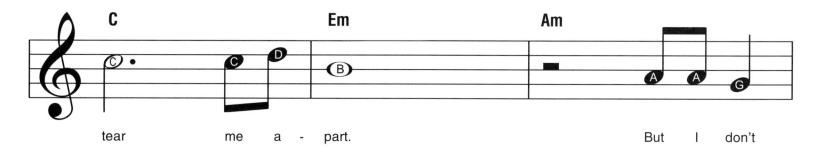

tear me a - part. But I don't

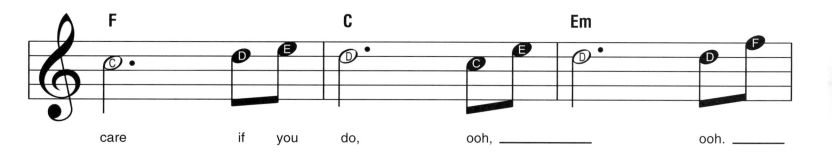

care if you do, ooh, _____ ooh. _____

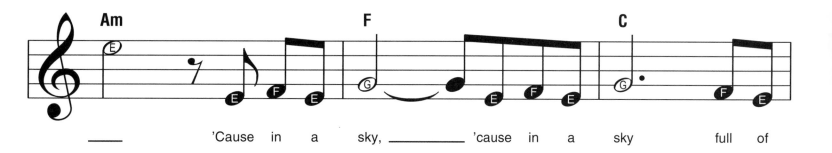

____ 'Cause in a sky, _____ 'cause in a sky full of

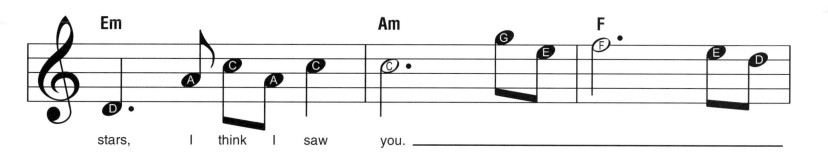

stars, I think I saw you. _____

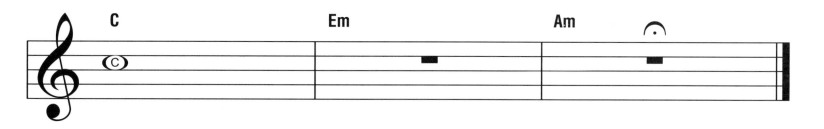

___

Some Nights

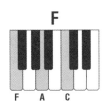
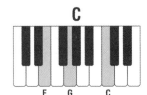
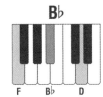
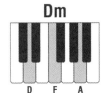

Words and Music by Jeff Bhasker,
Andrew Dost, Jack Antonoff
and Nate Ruess

Moderately

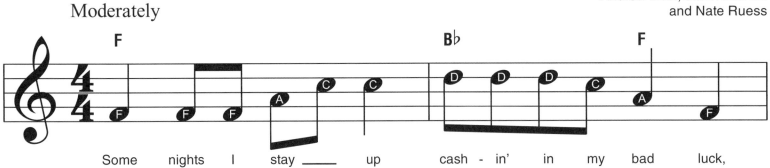

Some nights I stay ___ up cash - in' in my bad luck,

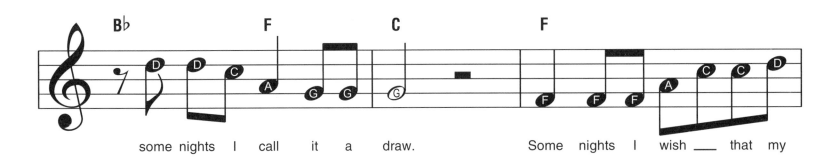

some nights I call it a draw. Some nights I wish ___ that my

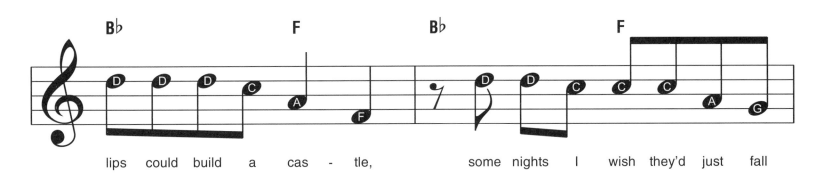

lips could build a cas - tle, some nights I wish they'd just fall

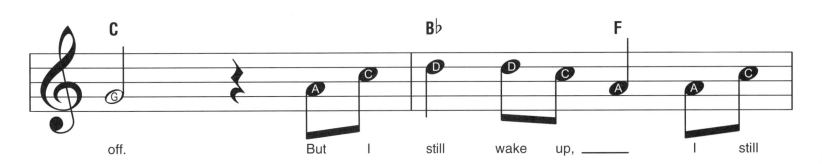

off. But I still wake up, _____ I still

Stay

Words and Music by Mikky Ekko
and Justin Parker

Stay with Me

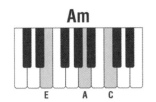
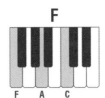
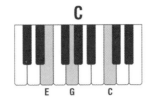
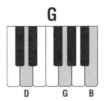
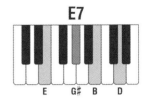

Words and Music by Sam Smith,
James Napier, William Edward Phillips,
Tom Petty and Jeff Lynne

Moderately slow

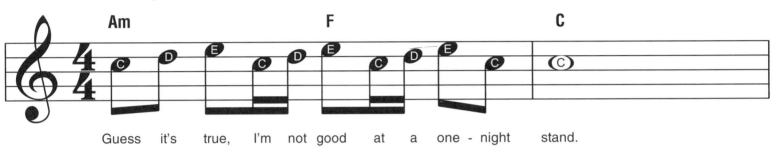

Guess it's true, I'm not good at a one - night stand.

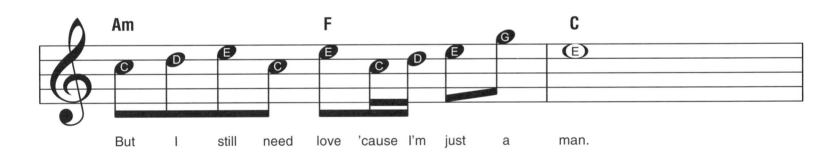

But I still need love 'cause I'm just a man.

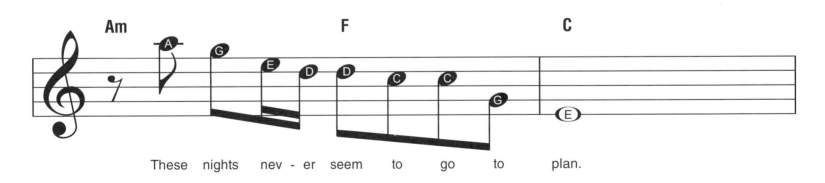

These nights nev - er seem to go to plan.

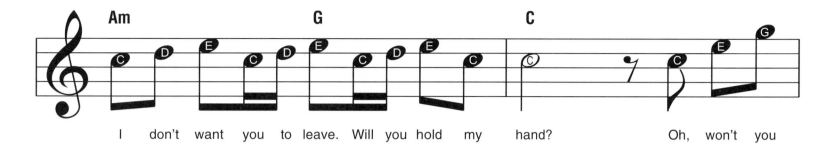

I don't want you to leave. Will you hold my hand? Oh, won't you

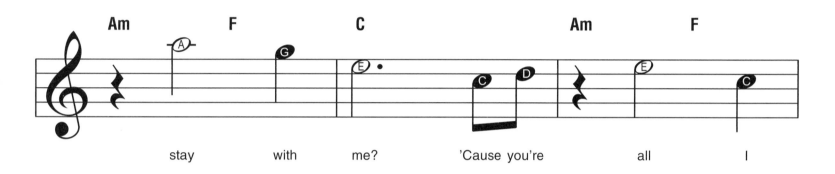

stay with me? 'Cause you're all I

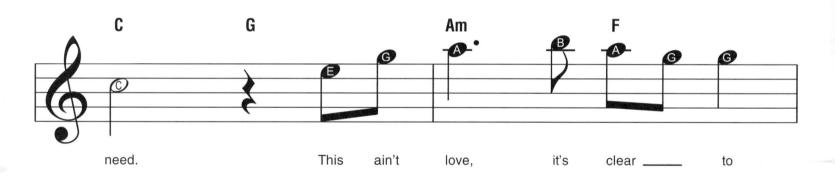

need. This ain't love, it's clear _____ to

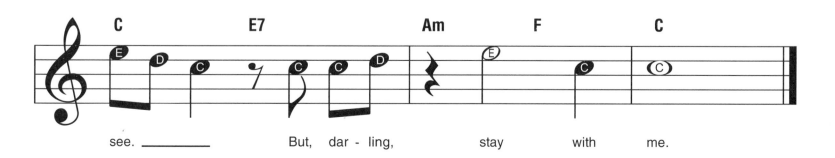

see. _____ But, dar - ling, stay with me.

Stitches

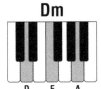
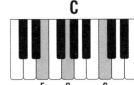
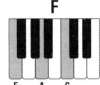

Words and Music by Teddy Geiger,
Danny Parker and Daniel Kyriakides

Moderately fast

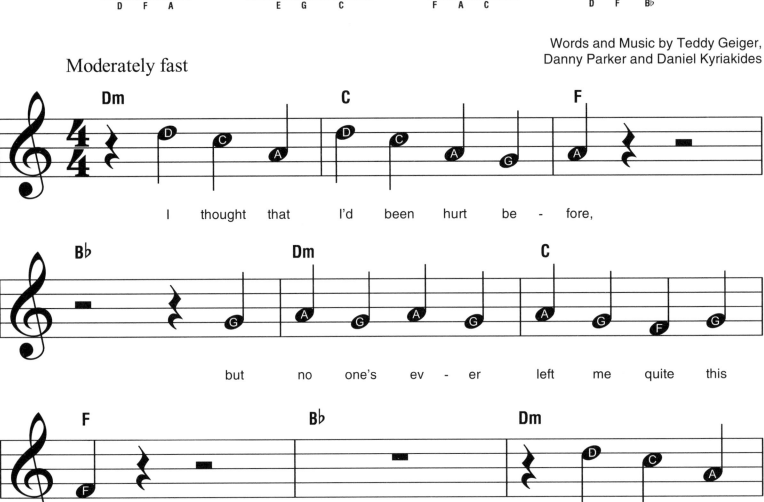

I thought that I'd been hurt be - fore,

but no one's ev - er left me quite this

sore.

Your words cut

deep - er than a knife.

Now I

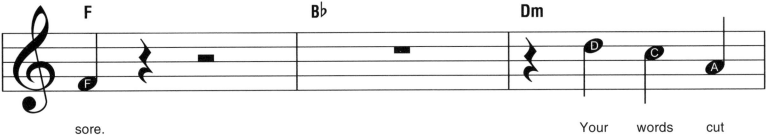

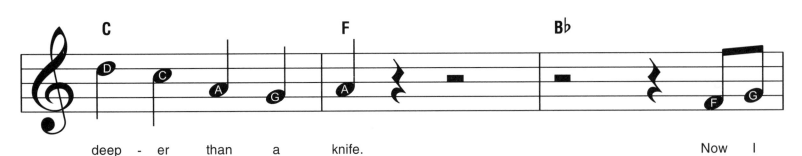

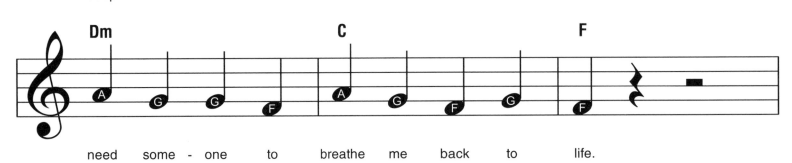

need some - one to breathe me back to life.

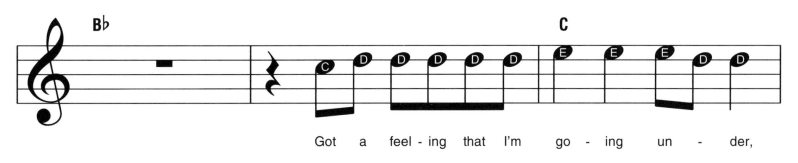

Got a feel - ing that I'm go - ing un - der,

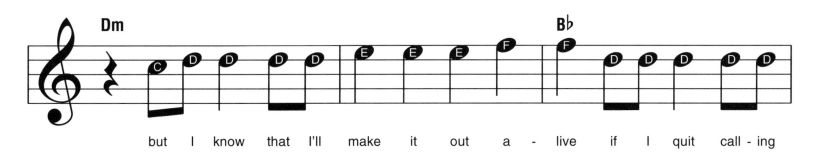

but I know that I'll make it out a - live if I quit call - ing

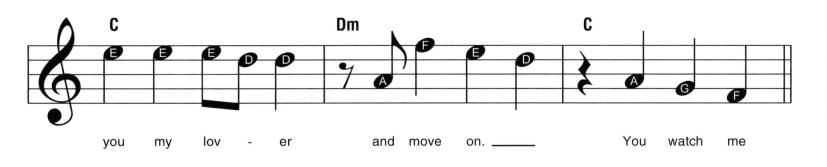

you my lov - er and move on. _____ You watch me

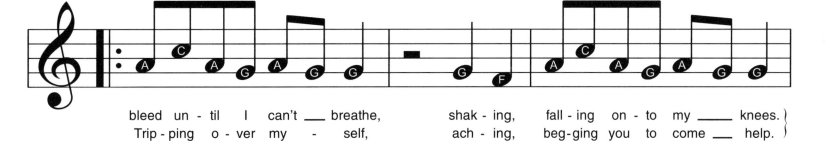

bleed un - til I can't __ breathe, shak - ing, fall - ing on - to my __ knees. ⎫
Trip - ping o - ver my - self, ach - ing, beg - ging you to come __ help. ⎭

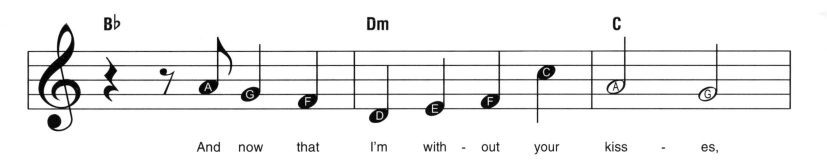

And now that I'm with - out your kiss - es,

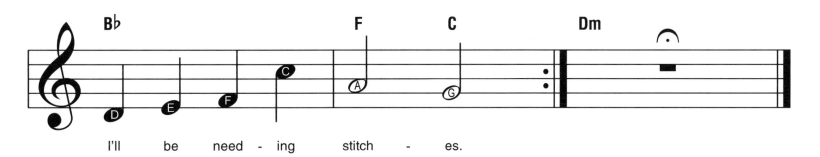

I'll be need - ing stitch - es.

Story of My Life

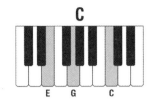
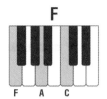
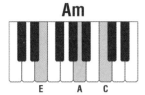

Words and Music by Jamie Scott,
John Henry Ryan, Julian Bunetta,
Harry Styles, Liam Payne,
Louis Tomlinson, Niall Horan
and Zain Malik

Moderately fast

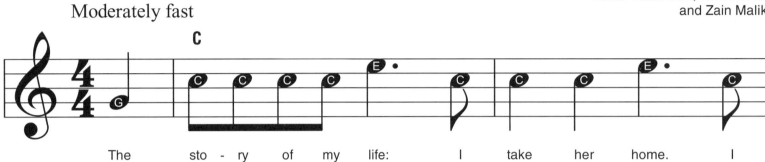

The sto - ry of my life: I take her home. I

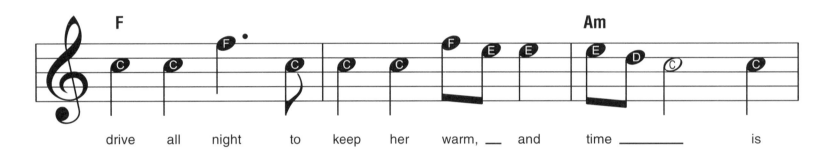

drive all night to keep her warm, __ and time __ is

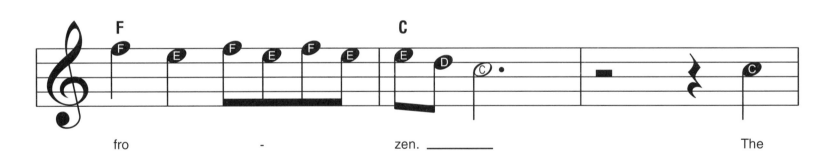

fro - zen. __ The

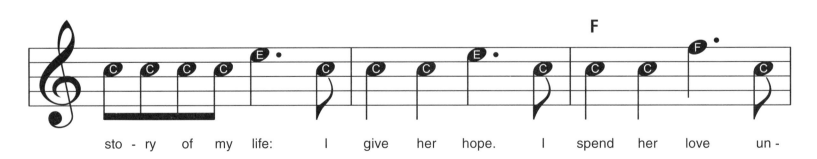

sto - ry of my life: I give her hope. I spend her love un -

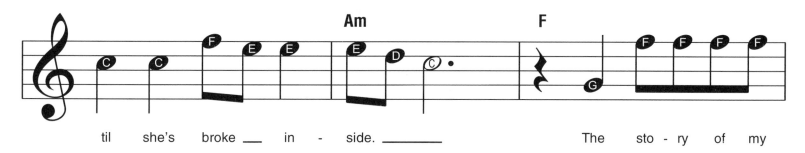

til she's broke ___ in - side. _____ The sto - ry of my

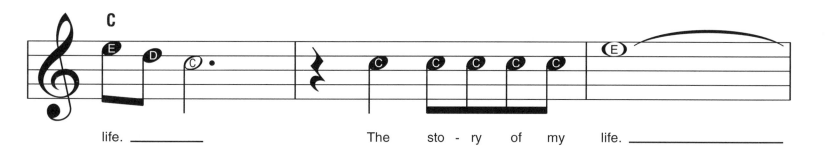

life. _____ The sto - ry of my life. _____

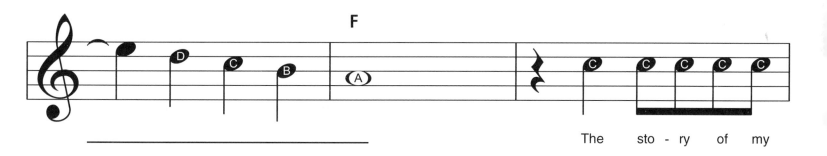

_____ The sto - ry of my

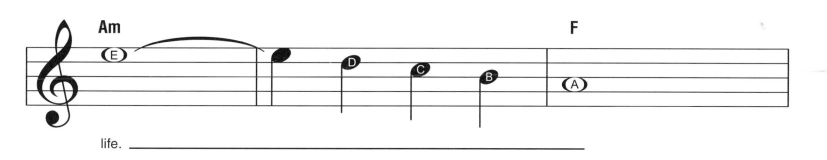

life. _____

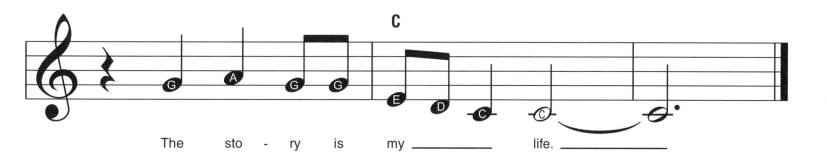

The sto - ry is my _____ life. _____

Take Me to Church

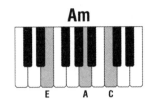
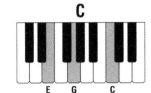

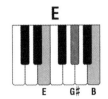

Words and Music by
Andrew Hozier-Byrne

Moderately slow

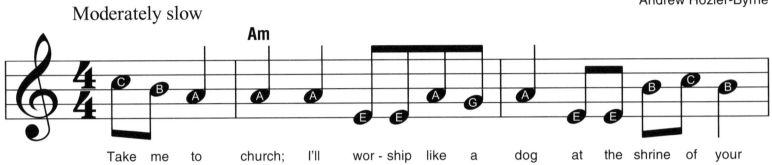

Take me to church; I'll wor - ship like a dog at the shrine of your

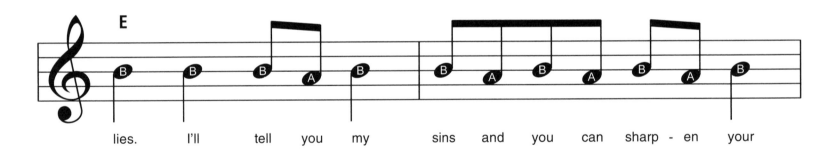

lies. I'll tell you my sins and you can sharp - en your

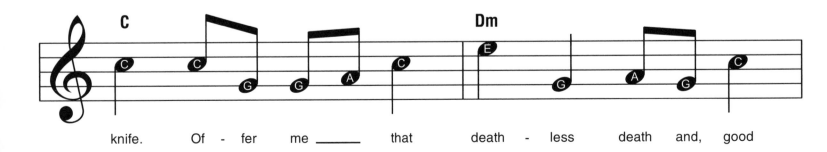

knife. Of - fer me _____ that death - less death and, good

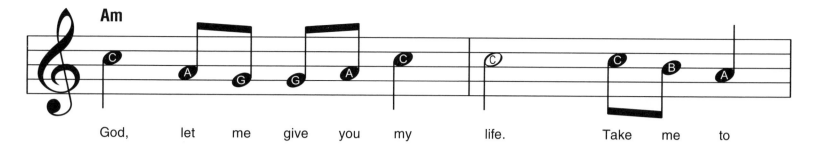

God, let me give you my life. Take me to

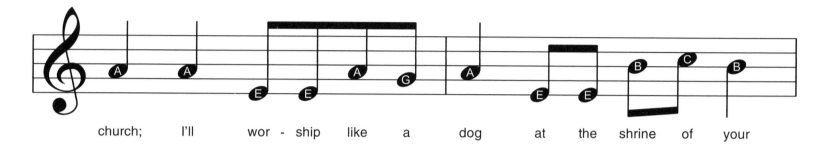

church; I'll wor - ship like a dog at the shrine of your

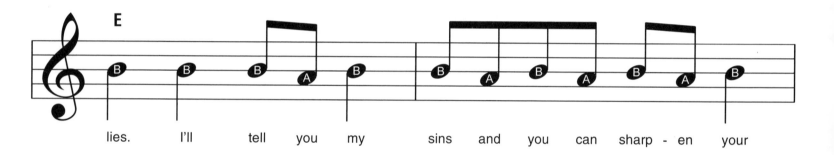

lies. I'll tell you my sins and you can sharp - en your

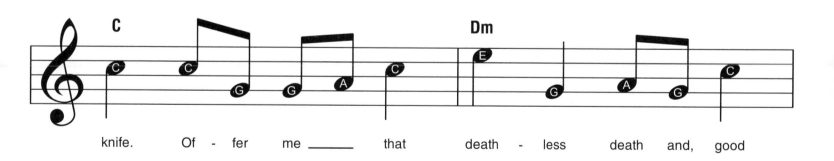

knife. Of - fer me ____ that death - less death and, good

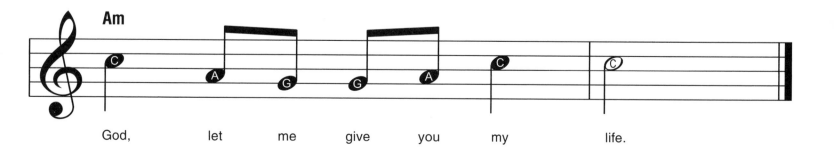

God, let me give you my life.

Tear in My Heart

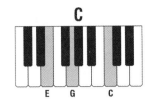
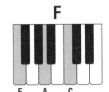
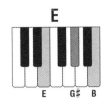
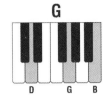
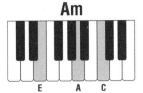

Words and Music by
Tyler Joseph

Moderately

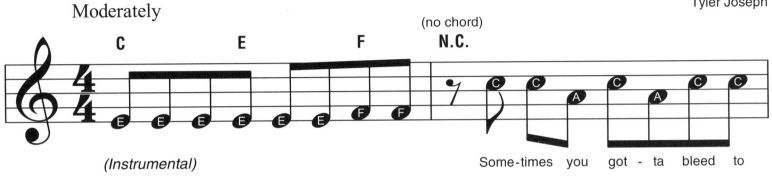

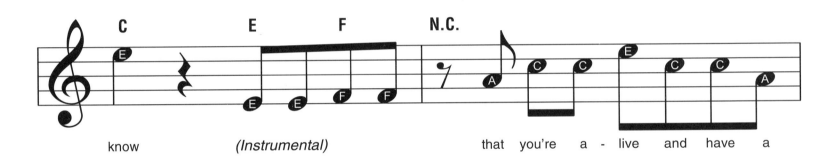

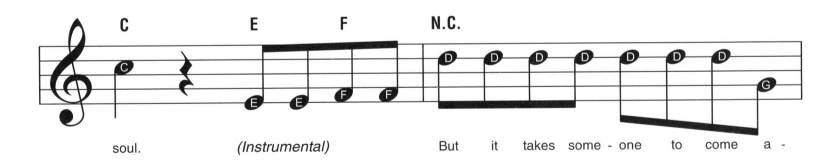

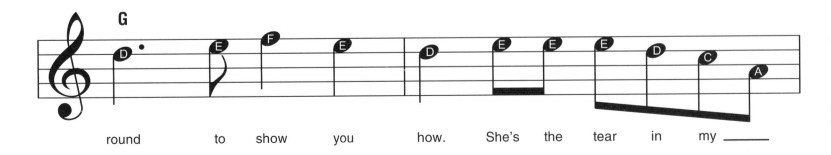

heart,   I'm a - live. _____ She's the tear in my _____

heart,   I'm on fi - re. She's the tear in my _____

heart,   take me high - er than I've ev - er been. My

heart   is my ar - mor. She's the tear in my _____

heart,   she's a carv - er. She's a butch - er with a

smile,   cut me far - ther than I've ev - er been.

Thinking Out Loud

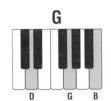
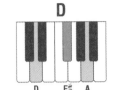
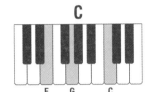
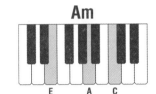
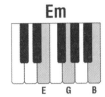

Words and Music by Ed Sheeran
and Amy Wadge

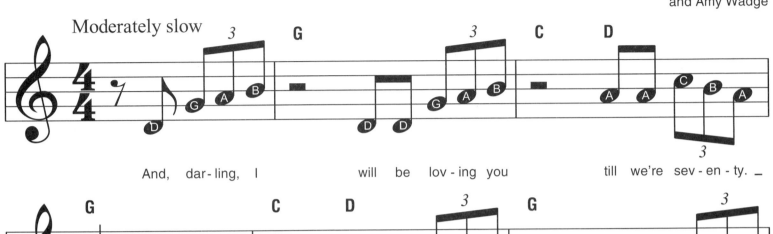

And, dar-ling, I will be lov-ing you till we're sev-en-ty. ___

___ And, ba-by, my heart could still feel as

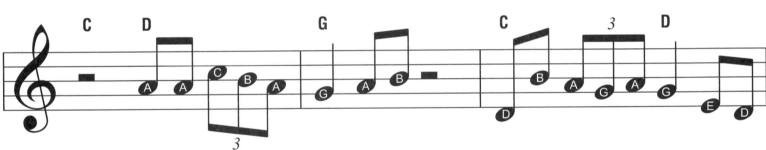

hard at twen-ty-three. ___ And I'm think-ing 'bout how ___

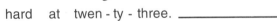
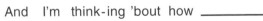

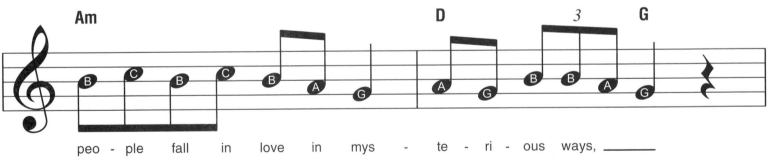

peo-ple fall in love in mys-te-ri-ous ways, ___

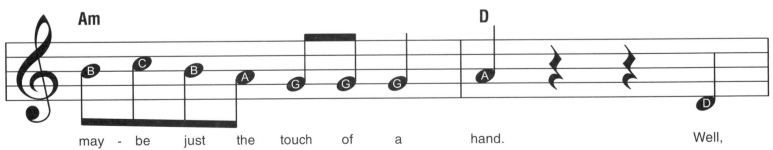

may-be just the touch of a hand. Well,

A Thousand Years
from the Summit Entertainment film
THE TWILIGHT SAGA: BREAKING DAWN - Part 1

Words and Music by David Hodges
and Christina Perri

Uptown Funk

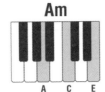
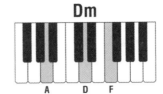

Words and Music by Mark Ronson,
Bruno Mars, Philip Lawrence,
Jeff Bhasker, Devon Gallaspy,
Nicholaus Williams, Lonnie Simmons,
Ronnie Wilson, Charles Wilson,
Rudolph Taylor and Robert Wilson

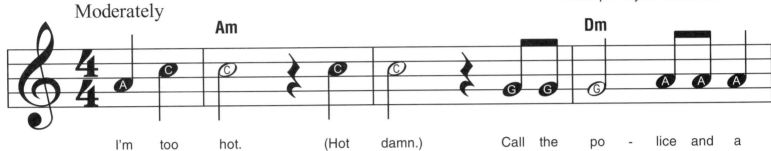

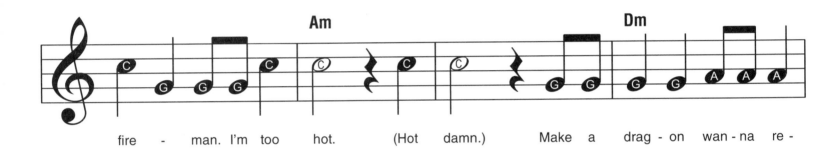

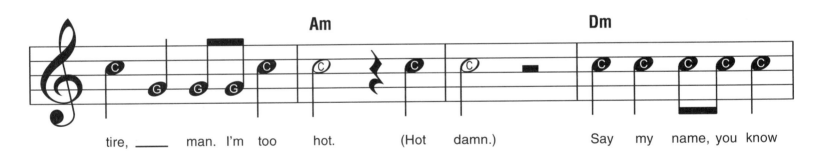

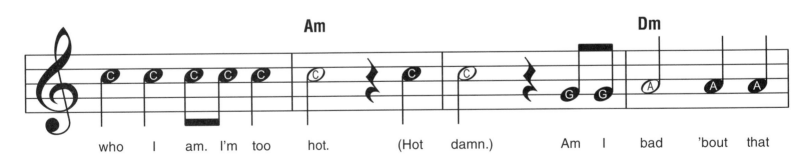

Viva La Vida

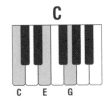 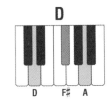 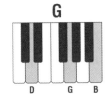 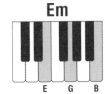

Words and Music by Guy Berryman,
Jon Buckland, Will Champion
and Chris Martin

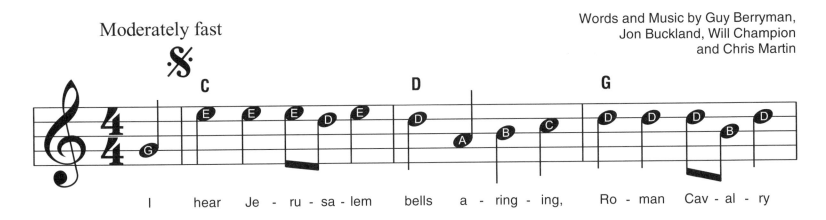

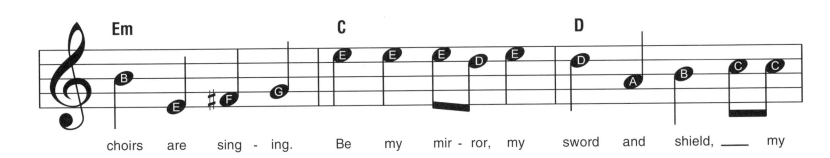

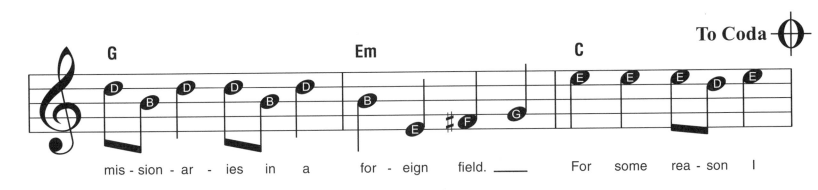

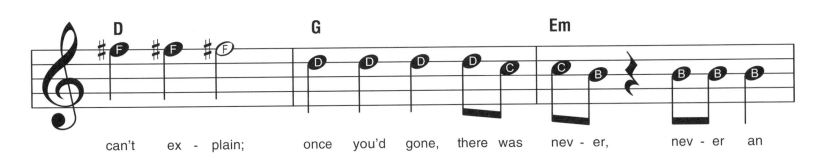

121

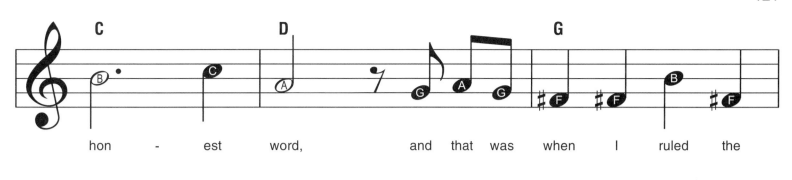

hon - est word, and that was when I ruled the

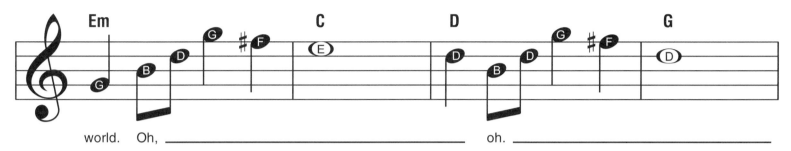

world. Oh, _____ oh. _____

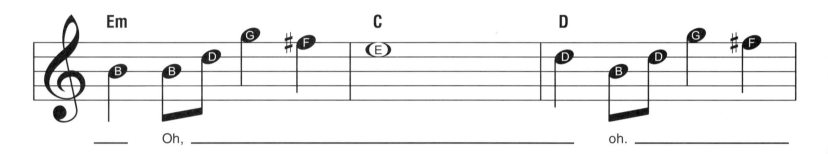

_____ Oh, _____ oh. _____

D.S. al Coda
(Return to 𝄋, play to ⨁
and skip to Coda)

CODA

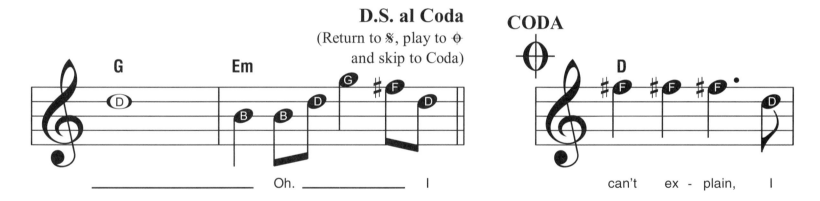

_____ Oh. _____ I   can't ex - plain, I

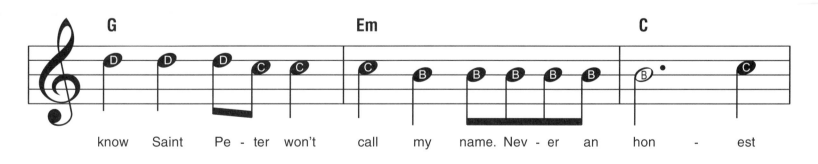

know Saint Pe - ter won't call my name. Nev - er an hon - est

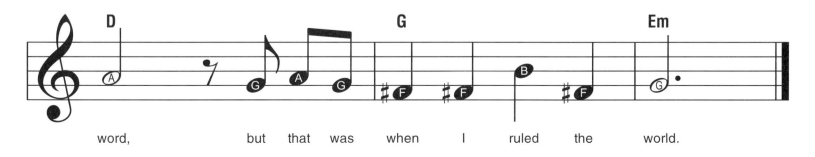

word,   but that was when I ruled the world.

The Walker

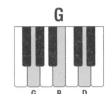 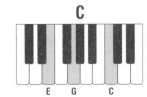 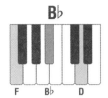 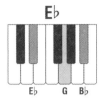

Words and Music by Michael Fitzpatrick,
Jeremy Ruzumna, Noelle Scaggs,
Joseph Karnes, James Midhi King
and John Meredith Wicks

Moderately fast

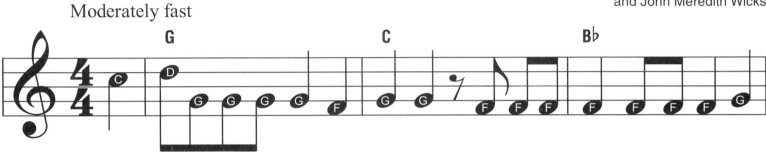

Ooh, cra-zy's what they think a-bout me. Ain't gon-na stop 'cause they tell me

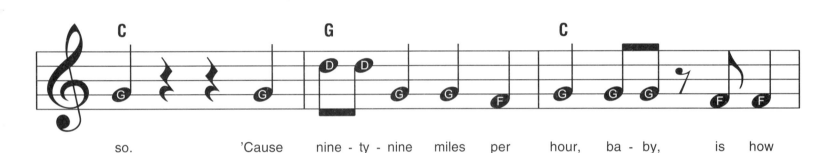

so. 'Cause nine-ty-nine miles per hour, ba-by, is how

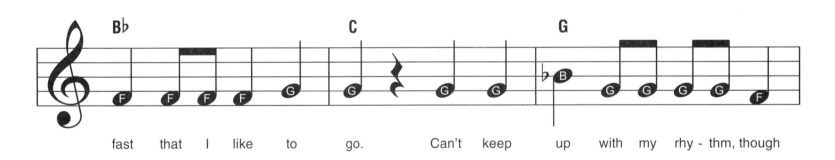

fast that I like to go. Can't keep up with my rhy-thm, though

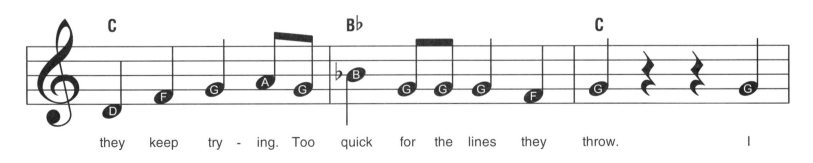

they keep try-ing. Too quick for the lines they throw. I

When I Was Your Man

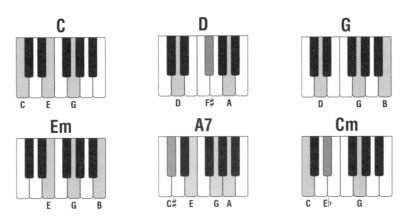

Words and Music by Bruno Mars,
Ari Levine, Philip Lawrence
and Andrew Wyatt

Moderately

I should-'ve bought you flow - ers and held your hand, should-'ve gave you all my ho - urs when I had the chance, take you to ev - 'ry par - ty, 'cause all you want - ed to do was dance. _____